AMERICAN SCHOOL OF NEEDLEWORK

PRESENTS

The Great CHRISTMAS Crochet Book

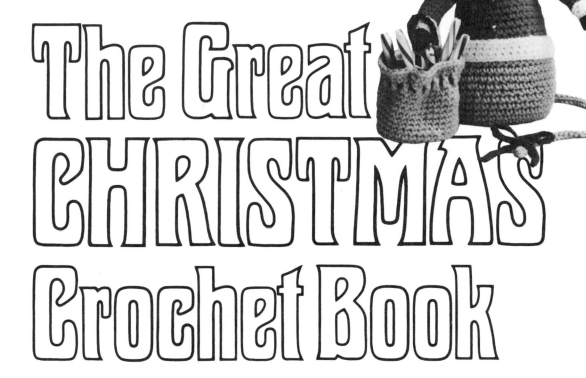

President: Jean Leinhauser
Director of Marketing and Book Coordinator: Rita Weiss
Editorial Director: Mary Thomas
Art Director: Carol Wilson Mansfield
Operations Vice President: Irmgard Barnes

Photography by Stemo Photography, Inc., Northbrook, Illinois
Roderick A. Stemo, President
James E. Zorn, Photographer

Book design by CBG Graphics
Carol Belanger Grafton, Designer

 Sterling Publishing Co., Inc.   New York

*We have made every effort to ensure the accuracy and
completeness of the instructions in this book.
We cannot, however, be responsible for human error,
typographical mistakes or variations in individual work.*

Copyright © 1981 by the American School of Needlework, Inc.
Published by Sterling Publishing Co., Inc.
Two Park Avenue, New York, N. Y. 10016
Available in Canada from Oak Tree Press, Ltd.
c/o Canadian Manda Group, 215 Lakeshore Boulevard East
Toronto, Ontario
Manufactured in the United States of America
All rights reserved
Sterling ISBN 0-8069-5452-3

Introduction

People celebrate Christmas in many different ways, but here, at the American School of Needlework, Christmas is celebrated in a unique fashion. Every year we create a new set of crochet patterns especially for the holiday season. It might be something as simple as a tree top angel, a set of Christmas ornaments or a project as elaborate as a complete set of Christmas carolers to decorate our Christmas table. Our designs seem to capture the warmth and love our staff experiences at Christmas.

Our Christmas stockings, for instance, have to be very large because we love to receive presents, and we have to design special items for our pets so that they can join in the Christmas celebration too. We love to design "Christmas Critters": giant snowmen, Christmas mice and huge Santas. And no Christmas is complete without some "sugar plums," those zanies that bring smiles to our faces like a Santa bib for a Christmas baby or a crocheted piece of holly to tie on a package or wear on a lapel. And because we remember Christmas as a special time for children, we design special Christmas toys for Santa to carry in his pack.

We've collected some of our favorite projects in this book (which we have printed in special easy-to-read large type), and we've included some new ones which we designed especially for this Christmas. Our chapters follow the lines of the famous poem, "A Visit from St. Nicholas" because the poem expresses our holiday spirit: a joyous occasion filled with fun and good cheer for everyone.

So from all of us, "Happy Christmas to all, and to all a good night!"

Jean Leinhauser

Jean Leinhauser
President
American School of Needlework, Inc.

ACKNOWLEDGMENTS

Several designs in this book were originally created by us for the American Thread Company, Stamford, Connecticut, and were copyrighted by them. It is with their kind permission that we are able to include those designs in this book.

To ensure the accuracy and clarity of our instructions, all of the projects in this book were tested by a group of dedicated and hardworking women, who made the designs which we have photographed. We express our appreciation to the following group of pattern testers:

Irene Beitner, Berwyn, Illinois
Judy Demain, Highland Park, Illinois
Eleanor Denner, Pontiac, Missouri
Kim Hubal, Evanston, Illinois
Joan Kokaska, Wildwood, Illinois
Barbara Luoma, Clearwater, Florida
Margaret Miller, Chicago, Illinois
Karen Moe, Buffalo Grove, Illinois
Patty Rankin, Minneapolis, Minnesota
Cindy Raymond, Vernon Hills, Illinois
Kathie Schroeder, Tucson, Arizona
Mary Thomas, Libertyville, Illinois

We also acknowledge our thanks and appreciation to the following contributing designers:

Winnie Ardito, Libertyville, Illinois
Joann Boquist, Chicago, Illinois
Eleanor Denner, Pontiac, Missouri
Anis Duncan, Northbrook, Illinois
Joan Kokaska, Wildwood, Illinois
Carol Wilson Mansfield, Northbrook, Illinois
Louise O'Donnell, Los Angeles, California
Sue Penrod, Loveland, Colorado
Barbara A. Retzke, Libertyville, Illinois
Kathie Schroeder, Tucson, Arizona
Mary Thomas, Libertyville, Illinois

Contents

Crochet Basics

Here's a quick review of the basics of crocheting, making pompons, plus a listing of all the abbreviations and symbols used in this book.

CROCHETING

CHAIN (ch)

Crochet always starts with a basic chain. To begin, make a slip loop on hook (**Fig 1**), leaving a 4″ tail of yarn.

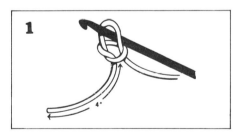

STEP 1: Take hook in right hand, holding it between thumb and third finger (**Fig 2**), and rest index finger near tip of hook.

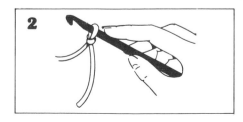

STEP 2: Take slip loop in thumb and index finger of left hand (**Fig 3**) and bring yarn over third finger of left hand, catching it loosely at left palm with remaining two fingers.

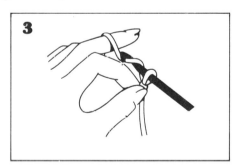

STEP 3: Bring yarn over hook from back to front (**Fig 4**), and draw through loop on hook.

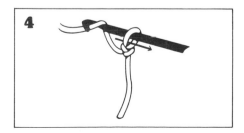

One chain made. Repeat Step 3 for each additional chain desired, moving your left thumb and index finger up close to the hook after each stitch or two (**Fig 5**).

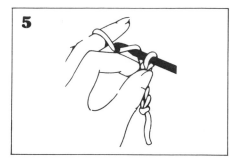

When counting number of chains, do not count the loop on the hook or the starting slip knot.

SINGLE CROCHET (sc)

First, make a chain to desired length.

STEP 1: Insert hook in top loop of 2nd chain from hook (**Fig 6**); hook yarn (bring yarn over hook from back to front) and draw through (**Fig 7**).

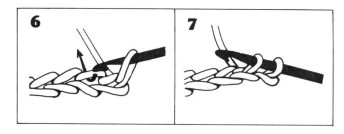

STEP 2: Hook yarn and draw through 2 loops on hook (**Fig 8**).

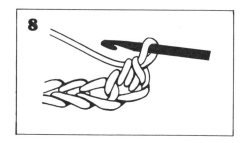

One single crochet made. Work a single crochet (repeat Steps 1 and 2) in each remaining chain.

To work additional rows, chain 1 and turn work counterclockwise. Inserting hook under 2 loops of the stitch (**Fig 9**), work a single crochet (as before) in each stitch across.

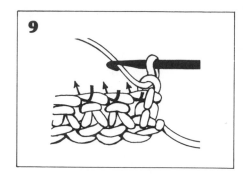

DOUBLE CROCHET (dc)

Double crochet is a taller stitch than single crochet. Begin by making a chain to desired length.

STEP 1: Bring yarn once over the hook; insert hook in the top loop of the 4th chain from hook (**Fig 10**). Hook yarn and draw through (**Fig 11**).

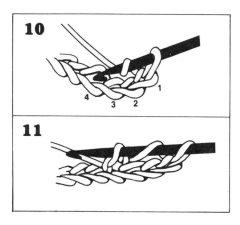

STEP 2: Hook yarn and draw through first 2 loops on hook (**Fig 12**).

STEP 3: Hook yarn and draw through last 2 loops on hook (**Fig 13**).

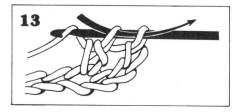

One double crochet made. Work a double crochet (repeat Steps 1 through 3) in each remaining chain.

To work additional rows, make 3 chains and turn work counterclockwise. Beginning in 2nd stitch (*Fig 14*—3 chains count as first double crochet), work a double crochet (as before) in each stitch across (remember to insert hook under 2 top loops of stitch). At end of row, work last double crochet in the top chain of chain-3 (*Fig 15*).

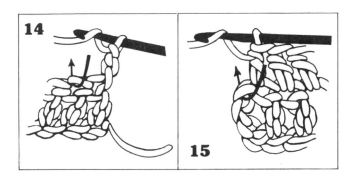

HALF DOUBLE CROCHET (hdc)

This stitch eliminates one step of double crochet—hence its name. It is taller than single crochet, but shorter than double crochet. Begin by making a chain to desired length.

STEP 1: Bring yarn over hook; insert hook in top loop of 3rd chain from hook, hook yarn and draw through (3 loops now on hook).

STEP 2: Hook yarn and draw through all 3 loops on hook (*Fig 16*).

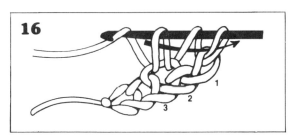

One half double crochet made. Work a half double crochet (repeat Steps 1 and 2) in each remaining chain.

To work additional rows, make 2 chains and turn work counterclockwise. Beginning in 2nd stitch (2 chains count as first half double crochet), work a half double crochet (as before) in each stitch across. At end of row, work last half double crochet in the top chain of chain-2.

TRIPLE CROCHET (tr)

Triple crochet is a tall stitch that works up quickly. First, make a chain to desired length.

STEP 1: Bring yarn twice over the hook, insert hook in 5th chain from hook (*Fig 17*); hook yarn and draw through (*Fig 18*).

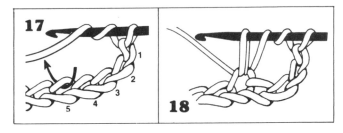

STEP 2: Hook yarn and draw through first 2 loops on hook (*Fig 19*).

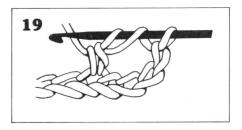

STEP 3: Hook yarn and draw through next 2 loops on hook (*Fig 20*).

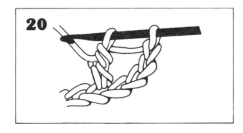

STEP 4: Hook yarn and draw through remaining 2 loops on hook (*Fig 21*).

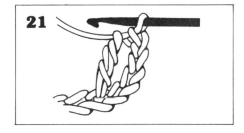

One triple crochet made. Work a triple crochet (repeat Steps 1 through 4) in each remaining chain.

To work additional rows, make 4 chains and turn work counterclockwise. Beginning in 2nd stitch (4 chains count as first triple crochet), work a triple crochet (as before) in each stitch across. At end of row, work last triple crochet in the top chain of chain-4.

SLIP STITCH (sl st)

This is the shortest of all crochet stitches, and usually is used to join work, or to move yarn across a group of stitches without adding height. To practice, make a chain to desired length; then work one row of double crochets.

STEP 1: Insert hook in first st; hook yarn and draw through both stitch and loop on hook in one motion. (*Fig 22*).

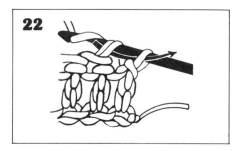

One slip stitch made. Work a slip stitch (repeat Step 1) in each stitch across.

ABBREVIATIONS

beg	begin(ning)
ch(s)	chain(s)
dc	double crochet(s)
dec	decrease (-ing)
EOR	every other row
fig	figure
hdc	half double crochet(s)
inc	increase (-ing)
lp(s)	loop(s)
patt	pattern
prev	previous
rem	remain(ing)
rep	repeat(ing)
rnd(s)	round(s)
sc	single crochet(s)
sk	skip
sl	slip
sl st(s)	slip stich(es)
sp(s)	space(s)
st(s)	stitch(es)
tch	turning chain
tog	together
tr	triple crochet(s)
YO	yarn over

work even: This term in instructions means to continue working in the pattern as established, without increasing or decreasing.

SYMBOLS

* An asterisk is used to mark the beginning of a portion of instructions which will be worked more than once; thus, "rep from * twice" means after working the instructions once, repeat the instructions following the asterisk twice more (3 times in all).

† The dagger identifies a portion of instructions that will be repeated again later in the pattern.

= The number after an equal sign at the end of a row/rnd indicates the number of stitches you should have when the row/rnd has been completed.

( ) Parentheses are used to enclose instructions which should be worked the exact number of times specified immediately following the parentheses, such as: (ch 3, dc) twice. They are also used to set off and clarify a group of sts that are to be worked all into the same sp or st, such as: (2 dc, ch 1, 2 dc) in corner sp.

[ ] Brackets and ( ) parentheses are used to provide additional information to clarify instructions.

GAUGE

It is essential to achieve the gauge—number of stitches and rows per inch—given in patt in order to make the correct size.

Before beginning your project, refer to the Gauge Note and make a gauge swatch using the hook and yarn specified. Work several rows; finish off. Place work on a flat surface and measure sts in center of piece. If you have more sts to the inch than specified, use a larger size hook. If you have less sts to the inch than specified, use a smaller size hook. Then make another gauge swatch and check your gauge once again. **Do not hesitate to change hook size to obtain the specified gauge.** Often you will not be able to achieve gauge with the size hook recommended.

While working, continue to check your gauge. Select sts/rnds near the center of your work, using small safety pins or straight pins to identify the sts to be measured and always measure over two or more inches.

POMPON

Cut 2 cardboard circles, each the diameter of finished pompon measurement, plus ½". Cut a hole in the center of each circle, approx ½" diameter. Thread a tapestry needle with 72" length of yarn, doubled. Holding both circles tog, insert needle through center hole, over outside edge, through center again until entire circle is covered. Thread more lengths of yarn as needed. (**Fig 23**)

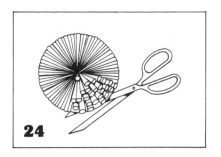

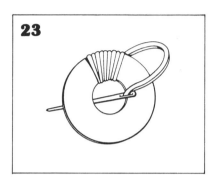

With very sharp scissors, cut yarn between the 2 circles all around the circumference (**Fig 24**). Using 12" strand of yarn doubled, slip yarn between circles, pull up tightly and tie very firmly. Remove cardboards and fluff out pompon by rolling it between your hands. Trim evenly with scissors.

NOTE: If diameter of pompon is less than 1", wrap yarn around tines of a dinner fork; then tie wrapped yarn securely between the center of the tines. Fluff and trim as for normal size pompon.

"Twas the night before Christmas..."

... and we're trimming our Christmas tree with wonderful crocheted ornaments, and when we're through we'll place our crocheted tree top angel on the top branch.

TREE TOP ANGEL

designed by Mary Thomas

This charming angel not only can top a tree, but can be a table decoration. For a centerpiece, make several in different hair shades and pastel-color dresses, stuff their skirts with tissue to make them stand alone.

Size

Approx 7″ tall

Materials

Sport weight yarn:
    1¼ oz blue
    ½ oz white
    4 yds yellow
Aluminum crochet hook size F (or size required for gauge)

Gauge

In sc, 9 sts = 2″; 6 rows = 1″
In Cone St, 3 sts = 1″; 3 rows = 1″

Pattern Stitch

CONE STITCH (abbreviated CS) To make a practice swatch, first ch 16.

Foundation Row: Work first CS as follows: YO, draw up ¼″ lp in 4th ch from hook; † sk one ch, draw up ¼″ lp in next ch (**Fig 1**); YO and draw through all 4 lps on hook, ch 1 † [first CS made]. * Work next CS as follows: YO, draw up ¼″ lp in same ch (where last CS was completed); rep from † to † once [one CS made]. Rep from * across, ending last CS in last ch, dc in last ch.

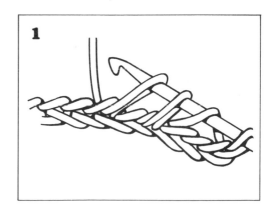

1

Patt Row: Ch 3, turn; work first CS as follows: YO, draw up ¼" lp in first sp (between dc and CS); † draw up ¼" lp in next sp (between CS), YO and draw through all 4 lps on hook, ch 1 † [first CS made]. * Work next CS as follows: YO, draw up ¼" lp in same sp (where last CS was completed); rep from † to † once [one CS made]. Rep from * across, ending last CS in last sp (between last CS and ch-3), dc in last sp.

Instructions

HEAD: Beg at top, with white, ch 2.

Rnd 1: Work 5 sc in 2nd ch from hook. Do not join; mark first st of rnd and move marker with each rnd.

Rnd 2: Work 2 sc in each sc around = 10 sc.

Rnd 3: *Sc in next sc, 2 sc in next sc; rep from * 4 times more = 15 sc.

Rnd 4: * Sc in each of next 2 sc, 2 sc in next sc; rep from * 4 times more = 20 sc.

Rnds 5 through 8: Work 4 rnds even in sc.

Rnd 9: *Sc in each of next 2 sc, decrease (dec) over next 2 sc [**To dec: Draw up a lp in each of 2 sts, YO and draw through all 3 lps on hook = dec made**]; rep from * 4 times more = 15 sc.

Rnd 10: * Sc in next sc, dec over next 2 sc; rep from * 4 times more = 10 sc. Before working next rnd, stuff head with yarn scraps.

Rnd 11: Dec 5 times = 5 sc.

Finish off, leaving 12" length. Thread into tapestry needle and weave through sts of last rnd. Draw up tightly and fasten securely, leaving end for sewing to dress later.

SLEEVES AND YOKE (*made in one piece*): First Half: Beg at center with blue, ch 18.

Row 1 (right side): Work CS Foundation Row (see Pattern Stitch instructions) = 7 CS.

Row 2: Ch 3, turn; work increase (inc) as follows: YO, draw up ¼" lp in dc; draw up ¼" lp in first sp (between dc and CS), YO and draw through all 4 lps on hook, ch 1 [inc made]; beg in same sp (where inc was completed) and work in CS Patt across (see Patt Row instructions) = 8 SC.

Rows 3 through 8: Rep Row 2, six times. At end of Row 8, change to white in last dc [**To change colors: Work st until 2 lps rem on hook, finish off blue; with white, YO and draw through 2 lps on hook = color changed**]. You should now have 14 CS.

Row 9: With white, rep Row 2 = 15 CS. Fold in half lengthwise with wrong sides tog; then join with a sl st in top of beg ch-3. Finish off.

Second Half: Hold piece just worked with right side facing you and Row 1 across top. Join blue with a sl st in first ch at upper right-hand corner; mark this ch for working skirt later.

Row 1: Ch 3, beg in same sp as joining and work same as Row 1 of First Half (you will be working CS in same chs where CS of First Half were worked).

Rows 2 through 9: Work same a First Half.

SKIRT: Hold folded Sleeves and Yoke piece with marked edge across top. Join blue with a sl st in marked ch [center back].

Rnd 1 (right side): Beg at center back, ch 3; work first CS in same ch as joining and in sp at end of next row; † work next CS in same sp (where last CS was completed) and in sp at end of next row †; †† work next CS (joining CS) in same sp (where last CS was completed) and in sp of corresponding row (2nd row from foundation ch) on opposite edge ††. Working across front: rep from † to † once; work next CS in same sp (where last CS was completed) and in ch of foundation ch; rep from † to † twice; rep from †† to †† once. Working across rem half of back: rep from † to † once; work last CS in same sp (where last CS was completed and in same ch where rnd was started); join with a sl st in top of ch-3 = 10 CS.

Rnd 2: Ch 3, turn; beg in sp between ch-3 and first CS and work 3 CS across back; † dc in same sp (where last CS was completed), ch 1 †; beg in same sp (where dc was worked) and work 4 CS across front; rep from † to † once; beg in same sp (where dc was worked) and work 3 CS across rem half of back, ending last CS in sp between last CS and ch-3; join with a sl st in top of ch-3 = 10 CS.

Rnd 3 (inc): Ch 3, turn; beg in sp between ch-3 and first CS and work in CS Patt across back, † ending in sp between CS and dc; work next CS in same sp and in dc; dc in same dc, ch 1; work next CS in same dc and in sp between dc and next CS †; beg in same sp and work in CS Patt across front; rep from † to † once; beg in same sp and work in CS Patt across rem half of back, ending in sp between last CS and ch-3; join with a sl st in top of beg ch-3 = 14 CS.

Rnd 4: Ch 3, turn; beg in sp between ch-3 and first CS and work in CS Patt across to dc, † ending in sp between CS and dc; dc in dc, ch 1†; beg in sp between dc and CS and work in CS Patt across front; rep from † to † once; beg in sp between dc and CS and work in CS Patt across rem half of back, ending in sp between last CS and ch-3; join with a sl st in top of beg ch-3 = 14 CS.

Rnds 5 through 12: Rep Rnds 3 and 4, four times. You should have at end of Rnd 5, 18 CS; at end of Rnd 7, 22 CS; at end of Rnd 9, 26 CS; at end of Rnd 11, 30 CS.

Rnd 13: Change to white; ch 3, turn; working in each sp around, work 32 CS; join with a sl st in top of beg ch-3. Finish off.

WINGS (*worked in one piece*): First Half: Beg at center with white, ch 8.

Row 1: Work CS Foundation Row = 2 CS.

Rows 2 through 6: Rep Row 2 of First Half of Sleeves and Yoke, 5 times. At end of Rnd 6, you should have 7 CS. Finish off.

Second Half: Hold piece just made with right side of Row 1 across top. Join white with a sl st in first ch at upper right-hand corner.

Row 1: Rep Row 1 of Second Half of Sleeves and Yoke.

Rows 2 through 6: Work same as First half of Wings. Finish off.

Finishing

Weave in all yarn ends. Sew last rnd of head to folded edge of Sleeves and Yoke at center. Sew wings to back of Sleeves and Yoke as shown in *Fig 2.*

Hair: Cut 20 strands of yellow 6″ long. Cut another strand of yellow 20″ long; use doubled and tie 20 strands tightly at center. With ends of same strand, sew center of hair to beg rnd of head having equal length and number of strands on each side of head. Tie strands tog at each side of head to folded edge of Sleeves and Yoke with 5″ strand of blue; knot securely and tie into a bow. Trim ends of hair and bow as desired.

Drawstring: With white, make a chain to measure approx 12″. Beg at front and weave through sts in Rnd 1 of Skirt. Knot each end of tie. Place angel at top of tree; then tie drawstring into a bow securing angel to a tree.

See page 23 for *Popcorn and Cranberry Garland* and page 119 for *Tiny Treasures* package ornaments.

16

COVERED TREE ORNAMENTS

designed by Mary Thomas

Shimmering satin tree ornaments take on a whole new look when covered in delicate crochet. These three patterns can be made either in perle cotton or baby weight yarn (both with an aluminum hook).

FILET ORNAMENT

Size

Approx 3″ diameter

Materials

Perle cotton #5:
  One ball red
[NOTE: Baby weight yarn may be substituted for perle cotton as shown in photo]
Aluminum crochet hook size E (or size required for gauge)
Bright gold satin ornament, 3″ diameter

Gauge

In dc, 5 sts = 1″; 4 rows = 1¼″

Instructions

Beg at top, ch 2. [NOTE: All rnds are worked on right side.]

Rnd 1: Work 6 sc in 2nd ch from hook, join with a sl st in beg sc.

Rnd 2: Ch 5, * dc in next sc, ch 2; rep from * 4 times more, join with a sl st in 3rd ch of beg ch-5.

Rnd 3: Ch 3, dc in same ch as joining; * ch 3, 2 dc in next dc; rep from * 4 times more, ch 3, join with a sl st in top of beg ch-3.

Rnd 4: Ch 3, dc in same ch as joining; 2 dc in next dc, ch 2; * 2 dc in each of next 2 dc, ch 2; rep from * 4 times more, join with a sl st in top of beg ch-3.

Rnd 5: Ch 3, dc in same ch as joining; * dc in each of next 2 dc, 2 dc in next dc; ch 1, 2 dc in next dc; rep from * 5 times more, ending last rep by joining with a sl st in top of beg ch-3.

Rnd 6: Ch 3, dc in each of next 5 dc; * ch 2, dc in each of next 6 dc; rep from * 4 times more, ch 2, join with a sl st in top of beg ch-3.

Rnd 7: Sl st into last ch-2 sp of prev rnd (before joining); ch 5, sk ch-3 and next dc; * dc in each of next 2 dc, ch 2; sk 2 dc, 2 dc in ch-2 sp; ch 2, sk 2 dc; rep from * 4 times more, dc in each of next 2 dc, ch 2; sk 2 dc, dc in ch-2 sp, join with a sl st in 3rd ch of beg ch-5.

Rnd 8: Ch 5, * dc in each of next 2 dc, ch 2; rep from * 10 times more, dc in last dc, join with a sl st in 3rd ch of beg ch-5.

Rnd 9: Sl st into next ch-2 sp; ch 3, dc in same sp; dc in each of next 2 dc, 2 dc in ch-2 sp; * ch 1, sk 2 dc; 2 dc in ch-2 sp, dc in each of next 2 dc; 2 dc in ch-2 sp; rep from * 4 times more, ch 1, sk last dc, join with a sl st in top of beg ch-3.

Rnd 10: Ch 3, dc in each of next 5 dc; * ch 1, dc in each of next 6 dc; rep from * 4 times more, ch 1, join with a sl st in top of beg ch-3.

Before working next rnd, insert ornament inside work bringing hanger out through center of first rnd; then continue by working rnds around ornament.

Rnd 11: Sl st in next dc; ch 3, dc in each of next 3 dc; * ch 2, sk next dc; sk ch-2 sp and next dc, dc in each of next 4 dc; rep from * 4 times more, ch 2, sk last dc, join with a sl st in top of beg ch-3.

Rnd 12: Sl st in next dc; ch 3, dc in next dc; * ch 1, sk next dc; sk ch-2 sp and next dc, dc in each of next 2 dc; rep from * 4 times more, ch 1, sk last dc, join with a sl st in top of beg ch-3.

Rnd 13: Sl st in next dc; ch 3, * sk ch-2 sp and next dc, dc in next dc; rep from * 4 times more, join with a sl st in top of beg ch-3.

Finish off, leaving 6″ end; thread into tapestry needle. Weave through sts of last rnd; draw up tightly and fasten securely. Weave in all ends.

TASSEL: Following Tassel with Decorative Cap instructions below make one tassel (wind perle cotton 70 times around 5″ length of carboard) with decorative cap and attach securely to last rnd of ornament.

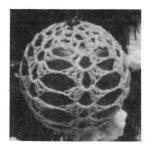

SHELL STITCH ORNAMENT

Size

Approx 3″ diameter

Materials

Perle cotton #5:
    One ball bright gold
[NOTE: Baby weight yarn may be substituted for perle cotton as shown in photo]
Aluminum crochet hook size E (or size required for gauge)
Red satin ornament, 3″ diameter

Gauge

In dc, 5 sts = 1″; 4 rows = 1¼″

Instructions

Beg at top, ch 2. [NOTE: All rnds are worked on right side].

Rnd 1: Work 6 sc in 2nd ch from hook, join with a sl st in beg sc.

Rnd 2: Ch 5, * dc in next sc, ch 2; rep from * 4 times more, join with a sl st in 3rd ch of beg ch-5.

Rnd 3: Work (ch 5, dc) in same ch as joining for beg shell; * work (dc, ch 2, dc) in next dc for shell; rep from * 4 times more, join with a sl st in 3rd ch of beg ch-5.

Rnd 4: Sl st into ch-2 sp of beg shell; ch 3, (dc, ch 2, 2 dc) in same sp; * (2 dc, ch 2, 2 dc) in ch-2 sp of next shell; rep from * 4 times more, join with a sl st in top of beg ch-3.

Rnd 5: Sl st in next dc and into ch-2 sp of beg shell; ch 3, (dc, ch 2, 2 dc) in same sp; * ch 1, (2 dc, ch 2, 2 dc) in ch-2 sp of next shell; rep from * 4 times more, ch 1, join with a sl st in top of beg ch-3.

Rnd 6: Sl st in next dc and into ch-2 sp of beg shell; ch 3, (2 dc, ch 2, 3 dc) in same sp; * ch 1, (3 dc, ch 2, 3 dc) in ch-2 sp of next shell; rep from * 4 times more, ch 1, join with a sl st in top of beg ch-3.

Rnd 7: Sl st in each of next 2 dc and into ch-2 sp of beg shell; ch 3, (2 dc, ch 2, 3 dc) in same sp; * ch 2, (3 dc, ch 2, 3 dc) in ch-2 sp of next shell; rep from * 4 times more, ch 2, join with a sl st in top of beg ch-3.

Rnd 8: Sl st in each of next 2 dc and into ch-2 sp of beg shell; ch 3, (2 dc, ch 2, 3 dc) in same sp; * ch 1, (3 dc, ch 2, 3 dc) in ch-2 sp of next shell; rep from * 4 times more, ch 1, join with a sl st in top of beg ch-3.

Before working next rnd, insert ornament inside work bringing hanger out through center of first rnd; then continue by working rnds around ornament.

Rnd 9: Sl st in each of next 2 dc and into ch-2 sp of beg shell; ch 3, (dc, ch 2, 2 dc) in same sp; * ch 1, (2 dc, ch 2, 2 dc) in ch-2 sp of next shell; rep from * 4 times more, ch 1, join with a sl st in top of beg ch-3.

Rnd 10: Sl st in next dc and into ch-2 sp of beg shell; ch 3, (dc, ch 2, 2 dc) in same sp; * (2 dc, ch 2, 2 dc) in ch-2 sp of next shell; rep from * 4 times more, join with a sl st in top of beg ch-3.

Rnd 11: Sl st in next dc and into ch-2 sp of beg shell; ch 3, dc in same sp; * 2 dc in ch-2 sp of next shell; rep from * 4 times more, join with a sl st in top of beg ch-3.

Rnd 12: Sl st in sp between ch-3 and dc; ch 3, * dc in sp between next 2 dc; rep from * 4 times more, join with a sl st in top of beg ch-3.

Finish off, leaving 6″ end; thread into tapestry needle. Weave through sts of last rnd; draw up tightly and fasten securely. Weave in all ends.

TASSEL: Following Tassel with Decorative Cap instructions below, make one tassel (wind perle cotton 70 times around 5″ length of cardboard) with decorative cap and attach securely to last rnd of ornament.

PUFF STITCH ORNAMENT

Size

Approx 2½″ diameter

Materials

Perle cotton #5:
    One ball white
[NOTE: Baby weight yarn may be substituted for perle cotton as shown in photo]
Aluminum crochet hook size E (or size required for gauge)
Red satin ornament, 2½″ diameter

Gauge

In dc, 5 sts = 1″; 4 rows = 1¼″

Instructions

Beg at top, ch 2. [NOTE: All rnds are worked on right side.]

Rnd 1: Work 8 sc in 2nd ch from hook, join with a sl st in beg sc.

Rnd 2: Pull up lp on hook to measure ½″; work puff st in same sc as joining [**To make puff st: (YO, draw up ½″ lp in st) 3 times, YO and draw through all 7 lps now on hook, ch 1 = puff st**

made]. *Ch 1, puff st in next sc; rep from * 6 times more, ch 1, join with a sl st in ch-1 at top of beg puff st. (NOTE: Join all following rnds in this manner unless otherwise specified). You should now have 8 puff sts.

Rnd 3: Pull up lp to 1/2"; puff st in same st as joining, ch 2; * puff st in ch-1 at top of next puff st, ch 2; rep from * 6 times more, join.

Rnd 4: Pull up lp to 1/2"; puff st in same st as joining, ch 3; * puff st in ch-1 at top of next puff st, ch 3; rep from *6 times more, join.

Rnd 5: Pull up to 1/2"; puff st in same st as joining, ch 4; * puff st in ch-1 at top of next puff st, ch 4; rep from * 6 times more, join.

Rnd 6: Rep Rnd 5.

Rnd 7: Rep Rnd 4.

Before working next rnd, insert ornament inside work bringing hanger out through center of first rnd; then continue by working rnds around ornament.

Rnd 8: Rep Rnd 3.

Rnd 9: Rep Rnd 2.

Rnd 10: Pull up lp to 1/2"; puff st in same st as joining, * puff st in ch-1 at top of next puff st; rep from * 6 times more, join.

Rnd 11: Ch 1, sc in same st as joining, sc in ch-1 at top of each rem puff st around, join with a sl st in beg sc.

Finish off, leaving 6" end; thread into tapestry needle. Weave through sts of last rnd; draw up tightly and fasten securely. Weave in all ends.

TASSEL: Follow Tassel with Decorative Cap instructions below and make one tassel (wind perle cotton 70 times around 5" length of cardboard) with decorative cap until cap measures approx 1". Do not finish off; complete cap as follows.

Puff St Rnd: Pull up lp to 1/2"; * puff st in next sc, sk one sc; rep from * 5 times more, join.

Last Rnd: Ch 1, 2 sc in same st as joining; 2 sc in ch-1 at top of each rem puff st around, join with a sl st in beg sc. Finish off and complete tassel as directed. Attach tassel securely to last rnd of ornament.

TASSEL WITH DECORATIVE CAP

Cut a piece of cardboard about 6" wide and as long as desired length of finished tassel. Wind yarn around length of cardboard the number of times specified in pattern instructions. Thread a tapestry needle with 20" length of yarn, doubled. Insert needle through all strands at top of cardboard, pull up tightly and knot securely, leaving ends for attaching to project. Cut yarn at opposite end of cardboard (**Fig 1**); remove cardboard.

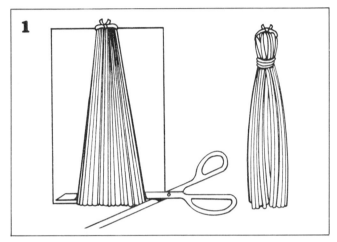

DECORATIVE CAP: Ch 2.

Rnd 1: Work 6 sc in 2nd ch from hook. Do not join; mark st at beg of rnd and move marker with each rnd.

Rnd 2: Work 2 sc in each sc around = 12 sc.

Rnd 3: Sc in each sc around. Rep Rnd 3 until cap measures approx 1 1/4". Join with a sl st in beg sc; finish off. Pull top of tassel through center of first rnd of cap. Trim end of tassel evenly with scissors.

SNOWFLAKES

Giant lacy snowflakes are a dramatic accent to hang in a window, a doorway, or on the tree. They work up quickly, and will be a treasured gift.

Sizes

Each snowflake measures approx 6″ from point to point.

Materials

American Thread Puritan Crochet Bedspread and Table Cotton:
250 yds White
Size 7 steel crochet hook (or size required for gauge)

NOTE: Approximately 80 yds of thread will make one snowflake.

Gauge

In sc, 8 sts = 1″

Special Techniques

TRIPLE CROCHET (abbreviated trc): (YO hook) twice, insert hook in st/sp and draw up a lp (4 lps now on hook: **Fig 1**); work (YO and draw through 2 lps on hook) 3 times = trc made.

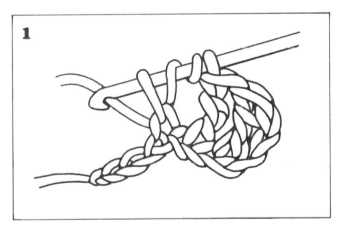

DOUBLE TRC: (YO hook) 3 times, insert hook in st/sp and draw up a lp (5 lps now on hook); work (YO and draw through 2 lps on hook) 4 times = double trc made.

TRIPLE TRC: (YO hook) 4 times, insert hook in st/sp and draw up a lp (6 lps now on hook); work (YO and draw through 2 lps on hook) 5 times = triple trc made.

RICE ST: Keeping last lp of each st on hook, work 3 trc in st/sp (4 lps now on hook: **Fig 2**); YO and draw through all 4 lps on hook = rice st made.

PICOT: Ch 4, sl st in 4th ch from hook = picot made.

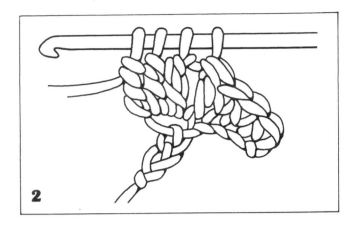

Finishing Techniques

Starching: After crocheting each snowflake, you'll need to starch it, using a thick solution of a commercial boilable starch (spray starches won't do the job) or a sugar-and-water starch that was traditionally used for old-fashioned doilies.

Sugar Starch: Mix ½ cup granulated sugar with ½ cup water in a small pan; heat to boiling (be careful not to burn mixture), immediately remove from heat. Cool to room temperature.

Wet snowflake in clear water, then immerse in starch. Remove from starch (very wet—don't wring out the starch) and place on a padded surface covered with clean, white paper. Insert rust-proof pins at points of snowflake, to hold tightly in shape. Evenly space a few pins along edges (between points). Let snowflake dry thoroughly (this may take several days in muggy weather) before removing pins.

Hanger: Use white or translucent nylon thread (or fishing line) to hang snowflake in desired location.

SNOWFLAKE NO. 1

Rnd 1: * Ch 5, work rice st (see Special Techniques) in 4th ch from hook; rep from * 5 times more. Join with a sl st in beg ch to form a ring, being careful not to twist sts = 6 rice sts.

Rnd 2: Work beg rice st as follows: Ch 4; keeping last lp of each st on hook, work 2 trc in same st as joining (3 lps now on hook), YO and draw through all 3 lps on hook (*beg rice st made*). In same st where beg rice st was just worked, work (ch 4, sl st, ch 4, rice st). * Ch 3; in ch between next 2 rice sts, work (rice st, ch 4, sl st, ch 4, rice st); rep from * 4 times more. Ch 3, join with a sl st in top of beg rice st.

Rnd 3: * Work (ch 5, rice st in 4th ch from hook) 3 times; sl st in top of next rice st, ch 3, sl st in top of next rice st; rep from * 5 times more, ending last rep by working sl st in beg ch (*before first rice st*).

Rnd 4: (*NOTE: Refer to Special Techniques for instructions to make picot, double trc and triple trc.*) Sl st in each ch up side of first rice st, then sl st in top of rice st. * Sc in ch between rice sts, ch 1; work (picot, ch 1) 4 times, sc in ch between next 2 rice sts. Work point as follows: Ch 2, work (picot, ch 1) 5 times; picot, dc in ch between 3rd and 4th picots from hook; picot, trc in ch between next 2 picots; picot, double trc in ch between next 2 picots; picot, triple trc in ch after next picot (*point completed*). Ch 2, sk next (rice st, ch-3, rice st); rep from * 5 times more. Join with a sl st in beg sc; finish off and weave in ends.

SNOWFLAKE NO. 2

Ch 4, join with a sl st to form a ring.

Rnd 1: Ch 8, dc in ring; * ch 5, dc in ring; rep from * 3 times more. Ch 5, join with a sl st in 3rd ch of beg ch-8 = 6 ch-5 sps.

Rnd 2: Ch 1, * work (sc, ch 3, sc) in next sp, ch 7; rep from * around. Join with a sl st in beg sc = 6 ch-7 sps.

Rnd 3: Ch 1, * 2 sc in next ch-3 sp, work (3 sc, picot—*see Special Techniques*—3 sc) in next ch-7 sp; rep from * around. Join with a sl st in beg sc.

Rnd 4: Ch 1, sc in same st as joining, * ch 3, sc in next sc; ch 15, sk next (3 sc, picot, 3 sc), sc in next sc; rep from * around, ending last rep by working sl st in beg sc to join (*instead of sc in next sc*).

Rnd 5: Ch 1, * sc in next ch-3 sp; in next ch-15 sp, work (4 sc, picot) 3 times, then work 4 more sc in same ch-15 sp; rep from * around. Join with a sl st in beg sc.

Rnd 6: Ch 8, sk first picot of next lp, work (dc, ch 5 dc, ch 5, dc) in center picot of same lp; ch 5, sk last picot of lp. * Dc in sc between lps; ch 5, sk first picot of next lp, work (dc, ch 5, dc, ch 5, dc) in center

picot of same lp; ch 5, sk last picot of lp; rep from * around. Join with a sl st in 3rd ch of beg ch-8.

Rnd 7: Ch 1, * work (2 sc, picot, 2 sc) in next ch-5 sp, 2 sc in next ch-5 sp. Work point as follows: Ch 4, 2 picots, ch 4; in 4th ch from hook, work (sl st, ch 3, sl st, ch 3, sl st) for tip of point; in ch at base of next picot, work (sl st, ch 3, sl st); then in ch at base of next picot, work (sl st, ch 3, sl st); ch 5 (*point made*). Work 2 sc in next ch-5 sp, work (2 sc, picot, 2 sc) in next ch-5 sp; rep from * around. Join with a sl st in beg sc; finish off and weave in ends.

SNOWFLAKE NO. 3

Ch 5, join with a sl st to form a ring.

Rnd 1: Ch 7, dc in ring; * ch 4, dc in ring; rep from * 3 times more. Ch 4, join with a sl st in 3rd ch of beg ch-7 = 6 ch-4 sps.

Rnd 2: Ch 1, work 6 sc in each sp around. Join with a sl st in beg sc.

Rnd 3: Ch 1, sc in same st as joining; work (ch 5, rice st in 5th ch from hook—*see Special Techniques*) twice. * Sk next 5 sc, sc in next sc; work (ch 5, rice st in 5th ch from hook) twice; rep from * 4 times more. Sk last 5 sc, join with a sl st in beg sc.

Rnd 4: Ch 4 (*counts as first trc*); * ch 5, rice st in 5th ch from hook; ch 2, trc in sp between next 2 rice sts; work 4 picots (*see Special Techniques*), ch 3 for tip of point; work 4 picots, sl st in top of last trc worked (*before picots were worked*); ch 7, rice st in 5th ch from hook; trc in sc between next 2 rice sts; rep from * 5 times more, ending last rep by working sl st in top of beg ch-3 to join (*instead of trc in sc between next 2 rice sts*).

Rnd 5: Ch 8, double trc (*see Special Techniques*) in same st as joining; ch 7, 5 dc in sp under ch-3 at tip of point, ch 7. * Work (double trc, ch 3, double trc) in next trc (*between rice sts*); ch 7, 5 dc in sp under ch-3 at tip of next point, ch 7; rep from * around. Join with a sl st in 5th ch of beg ch-8.

Rnd 6: Ch 1, * work (2 sc, picot, 2 sc) in next ch-3 sp, 7 sc in next ch-7 sp. Work loop in first dc at point as follows: Work (sl st, ch 4, double trc) in first dc at point; ch 5, sl st in top of double trc just made for picot; ch 4, sl st back into same (first) dc at point (loop made). Work loop in each of rem 4 dc at point, 7 sc in next ch-7 sp; rep from * around. Join with a sl st in beg sc; finish off and weave in ends.

POPCORN AND CRANBERRY GARLAND

designed by Joan Kokaska

Remember the nostalgic popcorn and cranberry garlands that used to highlight the Christmas tree? This contemporary version is crocheted—and will last from year to year (and is a lot less messy to make!). The unusual pattern stitch lets you make each garland just as long as needed.

Length

As desired

Materials

Worsted weight yarn
  for each yd length:
    ¾ oz white and 6 yds red
Aluminum crochet hook size I (or size required for gauge)

Gauge

In dc, 7 sts = 2″.

Instructions

* With white, † ch 3, work cluster in 3rd ch from hook [to make **cluster:** (YO and draw up ¾″ lp in st, YO and draw through 2 lps on hook) 4 times; YO and draw through all 5 lps now on hook, ch 1 = cluster made]. Turn cluster toward you until back of cluster is facing; sl st in same ch where cluster was just worked †. Rep from † to † 5 times, changing to red in sl st of last cluster [**To change colors: Insert hook in st, finish off color just used; hook new color and pull through = color changed**]. With red, rep from † to † twice, changing to white in sl st of last cluster. Rep from * for desired length. Finish off, weave in all ends.

"...when all through the house"

. . . we've decorated our home for the holiday season with crocheted wreaths, wall hangings and even a set of Christmas placemats with napkin rings.

REINDEER CHRISTMAS CARD HOLDER

designed by Joann Boquist

This whimsical reindeer, holding all of your holiday cards, will certainly brighten your house during the Christmas season. If you wish, you can eliminate the pocket and turn the reindeer into a wall hanging.

Size

Approx 20¼″ x 36″

Materials

American Thread Dawn Sayelle Knitting Worsted Size Yarn:
   8 oz each of Golf Green and Scarlet
   4 oz each of Copper and Sandstone
   2 oz Fisherman
   1 oz Flame
   ¼ oz Walnut
Sizes G and I aluminum crochet hooks (or size required for gauge)
22″ Dowel or curtain rod, ½″ diameter

NOTE: *Larger size hook is used for antlers, eyes and mouth only.*

Gauge

With smaller size hook, one square = 2¼″

Square Instructions

SOLID-COLOR SQUARE: With smaller size hook, ch 4, join with a sl st to form a ring.

Rnd 1 (right side): Ch 3, 2 dc in ring; * ch 1, 3 dc in ring; rep from * twice more. Ch 1, join with a sc in top of beg ch-3 (*brings yarn into position to start next rnd*).

Rnd 2: Ch 3, do not turn. Work 2 dc in sp under joining st (*beg corner*),* ch 1, work (3 dc, ch 2, 3 dc) in next ch-1 sp (*corner*); rep from * twice more. Ch 1, work 3 dc in beg corner sp; ch 2, join with a sl st in top of beg ch-3. Finish off, leaving approx 16″ sewing length.

DIAGONAL TWO-COLOR SQUARE: With smaller size hook and Color A, leave approx 20″ end—to be used later, ch 4, join with a sl st to form a ring. (*NOTE: For "Color A", use either color listed* for square; then for "Color B", use remaining color listed. When joining squares later, be sure to match colors with adjacent squares to form the picture.)

Rnd 1 (right side): Ch 3, carry beg yarn end (*lay yarn on top of ring and work following sts over it*); work (2 dc, ch 1, 3 dc) in ring, drop Color A (*do not cut*). With Color B, leave approx 72" end—to be used later, ch 1. Now carry both ends of Color A (*beg end and yarn from skein—do not carry 72" end of Color B*). Continuing with Color B, work (3 dc, ch 1, 2 dc) in ring; then work one more dc in ring, changing colors as follows: With Color B, work dc until 2 lps rem on hook; finish off Color B, leaving approx 4" end to weave in now or later; with beg end of Color A, complete st (YO and draw through both lps on hook). Drop beg end of Color A (*do not carry—will be used later*); with Color A (*from skein*), join with a sc in top of beg ch-3.

Rnd 2: Continuing with Color A, ch 3, do not turn; 2 dc in sp under joining st (*beg corner*); ch 1, work (3 dc, ch 2, 3 dc) in next ch-1 sp (*corner*); ch 1, 3 dc in next ch-1 sp; finish off Color A (*leave approx 4" end to weave in now or later*). Pick up Color B from behind work; ch 2, 3 dc in same sp (*corner completed*); ch 1, work (3 dc, ch 2, 3 dc) in next ch-1 sp (*corner*); ch 1, 2 dc in beg corner sp; work one more dc in beg corner sp, twisting colors as follows: With Color B, work dc until 2 lps rem on hook; pick up beg end of Color A from behind work, bring end up in front and then over strand of Color B and drop; with Color B, complete st (*YO and draw through both lps on hook*). Finish off Color B, leaving end for sewing length. With beg end of Color A, ch 2, join with a sl st in top of beg ch-3. Finish off, leaving end for sewing length.

QUANTITIES: Following Solid-Color Squares and Diagonal Two-Color Square instructions, make the following number of squares:

ONE-COLOR SQUARES	DIAGONAL TWO-COLOR SQUARES
10 Fisherman	2 Fisherman / Scarlet
4 Copper	6 Fisherman / Sandstone
18 Sandstone	4 Copper / Sandstone
41 Golf Green	6 Scarlet / Sandstone
66 Scarlet	4 Golf Green / Sandstone
	2 Golf Green / Scarlet

Assembling Squares

Position and join squares into two sections (wall hanging and pocket) as shown in *Fig 1*. To join, hold two squares with right sides tog. Carefully matching sts across, beg in ch st at corner and sew with overcast st **in outer lps only** (*Fig 2*) across

1

(pocket section)

APPLIQUE DETAILS

⊬ Antlers   ⅃ Mouth

◯ Eyes   Ᏺ Holly

◯ Nose

SOLID COLOR SQUARES

Color

Fisherman
Copper
Sandstone
Golf Green
Scarlet

DIAGONAL TWO-COLOR SQUARES

Colors	*Colors*
Fisherman/Scarlet	Scarlet/Sandstone
Fisherman/Sandstone	Golf Green/Sandstone
Copper/Sandstone	Golf Green/Scarlet

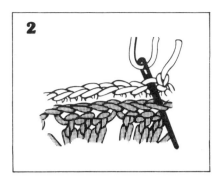

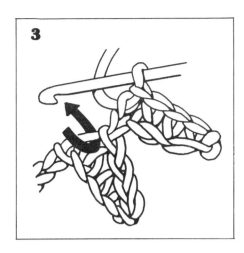

side, ending in ch st at next corner. You may join squares in rows across and then sew rows tog; or you may wish to sew squares forming parts of the picture, then sew these units tog. Be sure that all four-corner junctions are firmly joined.

When all squares have been joined into two sections, attach pocket section to wall hanging as follows: Place pocket section over Golf Green squares at bottom of wall hanging, having right side of each piece facing up. Carefully matching sts around outside edges, sew sections tog with overcast st **in outer lps only**. Then divide pocket into 3 equal sections of 6 squares each; use a running st and sew through both thicknesses at seam between each section.

To form top casing, fold over top squares to back of work and sew in place.

Applique Details

As each detail is completed, sew to wall hanging using matching sewing thread (refer to *Fig 1* for positions).

RIGHT ANTLER: (*NOTE: Wrong side of sts will be facing up when antler is sewn to wall hanging.*) Working up side of antler, with larger size hook and one strand each of Sandstone and Copper, ch 22. Sl st in 2nd ch from hook, (sk one ch, sl st in next ch) twice, sl st in next ch (*first branch made*). Ch 18; sl st in 2nd ch from hook, sk one ch, sl st in each of next 2 chs; sk one ch, sl st in next ch (*branch made*). Ch 22; sl st in 2nd ch from hook, sk one ch, sl st in each of next 2 chs (*branch made*).

Now work "V" at tip of antler. Ch 19; sc in 2nd ch from hook and in each of next 4 chs, sk one ch, sc in each of next 3 chs; ch 10, sc in 2nd ch from hook and in each of next 8 chs.

Working down opposite side of antler, 2 sc in side of next sc (*Fig 3*), sc in each of next 9 unused chs to next branch; sc in ch at base of branch, sc in each of next 5 chs. Ch 5, sl st in 2nd ch from hook and in each of next 3 chs (*branch made*). Sc in each of next 12 unused chs (*do not work first st in side of next sc*) to next branch; sc in ch at base of branch, sc in each

of next 3 chs. Ch 4, sl st in 2nd ch from hook and in each of next 2 chs (*branch made*). Sc in each of next 8 unused chs to next branch; sc in ch at base of branch, sc in each of next 3 chs. Ch 5, sl st in 2nd ch from hook and in each of next 3 chs (*last branch made*). Sc in each of rem 12 unused chs. Finish off; weave in ends. Sew to wall hanging, having wrong side of sts facing up.

LEFT ANTLER: With larger size hook and one strand each of Sandstone and Copper, ch 19. Sl st in 2nd ch from hook, (sk one ch, sl st in next ch) twice, sl st in next ch (*first branch made*). Ch 17; sl st in 2nd ch from hook, sk one ch, sl st in each of next 2 chs (*branch made*). Ch 23; sl st in 2nd ch from hook, (sk one ch, sl st in next ch) twice, sl st in next ch (*branch completed*).

Work "V" at tip of antler as follows: Ch 25, sc in 2nd ch from hook and in each of next 4 chs, sk one ch, sc in each of next 3 chs; ch 10, sc in 2nd ch from hook and in each of next 8 chs.

Working down opposite side of antler, 2 sc in side of next sc (*Fig 3*), sc in each of next 9 unused chs. Ch 4, sl st in 2nd ch from hook and in each of next 2 chs (*branch made*). Sc in each of next 6 unused chs to next branch; sc in ch at base of branch, sc in each of next 12 chs. Ch 5, sl st in 2nd ch from hook and in each of next 3 chs (*branch made*). Sc in each of next 4 unused chs to next branch; sc in ch at base of branch, sc in each of next 9 chs. Ch 6, sl st in 2nd ch from hook and in each of next 4 chs (*last branch made*). Sc in each of next 3 unused chs to last branch; sc in ch at base of branch, sc in each of rem 12 chs. Finish off; weave in ends. Sew to wall hanging in same manner as other antler.

EYES (*make 2*): With larger size hook and Walnut, ch 3, join with a sl st to form a ring.

Rnd 1: Work 8 hdc in ring; do not join.

Rnd 2: Do not turn; work hdc in each hdc around, join with a sl st in beg hdc. Ch 3, finish off; weave in ends. Sew to reindeer, having wrong side of sts facing up.

NOSE: With Flame, make 1½″ diameter pompon (see instructions on page 11).

MOUTH: With larger size hook and Walnut, make a chain to measure approx 9″ long; finish off. Sew to reindeer, having wrong side of chain facing up.

Holly

Sew 5 groups of 3 leaves and 3 berries each to Golf Green squares around neck of reindeer.

LEAVES (*make 15*): With smaller size hook and Golf green, ch 11. **Working in top lp of each ch,** sl st in 2nd ch from hook, sc in next ch; hdc in next ch, dc in next ch. Work picot as follows: Ch 3, sl st in 3rd ch from hook (picot made). Sc in next ch, hdc in next ch; dc in next ch, picot, sc in next ch; sl st in next ch, 3 sl sts in last ch. **Continuing to work on opposite side of starting chain,** sl st in next st, sc in next st; dc in next st, picot, sc in next st, hdc in next st; dc in next st, picot, sc in next st, sl st in each of last 3 sts. Finish off: weave in ends (*or if sewing length is desired, leave approx 6″ end*).

BERRIES (*make 15*): With smaller size hook and Flame, ch 2.

Rnd 1: Work 6 sc in 2nd ch from hook, do not join, work continuous rnds.

Rnd 2: Sc in each sc around.

Rnd 3: Rep Rnd 2. Finish off, leaving approx 6″ sewing length. Thread into tapestry or yarn needle and weave through sts of last rnd. Draw up tightly and fasten securely.

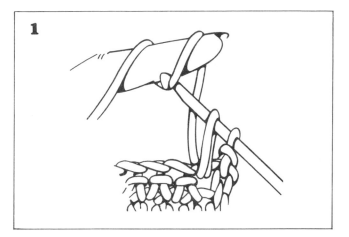

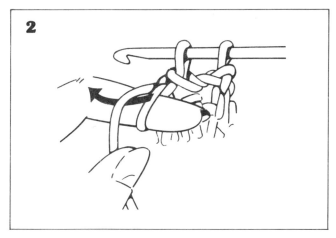

CHRISTMAS WREATH

Size

Approx 13″ diameter

Materials

Aunt Lydia's Heavy Rug Yarn in 70-yd skeins:
    3 skeins Spring Green
    3 skeins Grass Green
Aluminum crochet hook size J (or size required for gauge)
1½ yds red grosgrain ribbon, 2″ wide
12″ diameter styrofoam ring

Gauge

5 sc = 2″

Pattern Stitch

FRONT LOOP STITCH (abbreviated flp): With right side of work facing, insert hook into st; hook yarn and draw a lp through st (2 lps now on hook). Wrap yarn twice around tip of left index finger; insert hook in front of yarn and through first lp on finger (**Fig 1**), draw lp through one lp on hook. Bring left index finger down in front of work; skip first lp on finger and insert hook through 2nd lp on finger (**Fig 2**), draw lp through both lps rem on hook. Drop long lp off finger. One flp made.

Instructions

With one strand each Spring Green and Grass Green held tog (now and throughout), ch 17.

Row 1: Sc in 2nd ch from hook and in each rem ch across = 16 sc.

Row 2: Ch 1, turn; make a flp in each sc to last sc, sc in last sc.

Row 3: Ch 1, turn; sc in each st across. Rep Rows 2 and 3 until piece measures 32½″ or length equal to circumference of styrofoam ring. Fold in half and sl st across last row completed and first row, carefully matching sts. Place piece around ring and sew long edges tog securely.

Finishing

Make a ribbon bow and attach to wreath where first and last row were joined.

SET THE CHRISTMAS TABLE

CHRISTMAS TABLE RUNNER

designed by Mary Thomas

Size

Approx 12″ x 36″

Materials

Sport weight yarn:
    4 oz white
Size D aluminum crochet hook (or size required for gauge)

Gauge

In dc, 9 sts = 2″; 5 rows = 2″

Instructions

Ch 166 loosely. *(NOTE: Ch 3 counts as one dc.)*

Row 1: Dc in 4th ch from hook and in each rem ch across = 164 dc (counting ch-3).

Row 2: Ch 3, turn; dc in each of next 3 dc, * ch 4, sk 4 dc, dc in each of next 4 dc; rep from * across.

Row 3: Ch 3, turn; * dc in each of next 2 dc, ch 1; sk one dc, dc in each of next 4 chs; dc in each of next 4 dc, dc in each of next 4 chs; ch 1, sk one dc; rep from * across, ending dc in each of last 3 dc.

Row 4: Ch 3, turn; * dc in each of next 2 dc, ch 3; sk next dc, dc in each of next 10 dc; ch 3, sk next dc; rep from * across, ending dc in each of last 3 dc.

Row 5: Ch 3, turn; * dc in each of next 2 dc, ch 4; sk next dc, dc in each of next 8 dc; ch 4, sk next dc; rep from * across, ending dc in each of last 3 dc.

Row 6: Ch 3, turn; * dc in each of next 2 dc, ch 5; sk next dc, dc in each of next 6 dc; ch 5, sk next dc; rep from * across, ending dc in each of last 3 dc.

Row 7: Ch 3, turn; * dc in each of next 2 dc, ch 6; sk next dc, dc in each of next 4 dc, ch 6; sk next dc; rep from * across, ending dc in each of last 3 dc.

Row 8: Ch 3, turn; * dc in each of next 2 dc, dc in first ch of ch-6; ch 5, sk next dc, dc in each of next 2 dc, ch 5; sk next dc, dc in last ch of ch-6; rep from * across, ending dc in each of last 3 dc.

Row 9: Ch 3, turn; * dc in next dc and in each dc and each ch across = **164 dc.**

Row 10: Ch 3, turn; dc in next dc and in each dc across.

Rows 11 through 22: Rep Row 10 twelve times.

Row 23: Ch 3, turn; dc in each of next 3 dc, * ch 6, sk 5 dc, dc in each of next 2 dc; ch 6; sk 5 dc, dc in each of next 4 dc; rep from * across.

Row 24: Ch 3, turn; * dc in each of next 2 dc, ch 6; sk one dc, dc in last ch of ch-6, dc in each of next 2 dc, dc in first ch of next ch-6, ch 6, sk next dc; rep from * across, ending dc in each of last 3 dc.

Row 25: Ch 3, turn; * dc in each of next 2 dc, ch 5, dc in last ch of ch-6; dc in each of next 4 dc, dc in first ch of ch-6, ch 5; rep from * across, ending dc in each of last 3 dc.

Row 26: Ch 3, turn; * dc in each of next 2 dc, ch 4, dc in last ch of ch-5, dc in each of next 6 dc, dc in first ch of ch-5, ch-4; rep from * across, ending dc in each of last 3 dc.

Row 27: Ch 3, turn; * dc in each of next 2 dc, ch 3, dc in last ch of ch-4; dc in each of next 8 dc, dc in first ch of ch-4, ch 3; rep from * across, ending dc in each of last 3 dc.

Row 28: Ch 3, turn; * dc in each of next 2 dc, ch 1, dc in last ch of ch-3, dc in each of next 10 dc, dc in first ch of ch-3, ch 1; rep from * across, ending dc in each of last 3 dc.

Row 29: Ch 3, turn; * dc in each of next 2 dc, dc in ch-1; ch 4, sk 4 dc, dc in each of next 4 dc; ch 4, sk 4 dc, dc in ch-1; rep from * across, ending dc in each of last 3 dc.

Row 30: Rep Row 9. Finish off, weave in yarn ends.

CHRISTMAS PLACEMAT

designed by Mary Thomas

Size

Approx 12″ x 18″

Materials

Sport weight yarn:
    2 oz green
Aluminum crochet hook size D (or size required for gauge).

Gauge

Same as Table Runner

Instructions

Ch 86 loosely.

Row 1: Dc in 4th ch from hook and in each rem ch across = 84 dc (counting Tch as one dc).

Rows 2 through 30: Work Rows 2 through 30 of instructions for Table Runner.

CHRISTMAS NAPKIN RING WITH HOLLY APPLIQUE

designed by Kathie Schroeder and Mary Thomas

Materials

Sport weight yarn:
    ¼ oz white
    few yds each red and green
Aluminum crochet hook size D

Gauge

None specified

Instructions

With 2 strands of white ch 7.

Foundation Row: Sc in 2nd ch from hook and in each rem ch across = 6 sc.

Row 1: Ch 1, turn; sc in each sc across. Rep Row 1 until piece measures approx 4″.

Buttonhole Row: Ch 1, turn; sc in each of first 2 sc, ch 4, sk 2 sc, sc in each of rem 2 sc. Finish off; weave in yarn ends.

BERRIES (*make 2*): With single strand of red, ch 2.

Rnd 1: Work 6 sc in 2nd ch from hook.

Rnds 2 and 3: Sc in each sc around. Cut yarn, leaving approx 6″ end; thread into tapestry needle. Weave through sts of last rnd and draw up tightly; fasten securely, leaving yarn end for sewing.

LEAVES (*Make 2*): With single strand of green, ch 11. Working in one lp only of each ch across, sl st in 2nd ch from hook, sc in next ch, hdc in next ch; †dc in next ch, ch 3, sl st in first ch of ch-3 just made †; sc in next sc, hdc in next ch, rep from † to † once; sc in next ch, sl st in next ch, 3 sl sts in last ch. Turning piece slightly, continue by working on opposite side of starting ch: sl st in first ch, sc in next ch, rep from † to † once; sc in next ch, hdc in next ch; rep from † to † once, sc in next ch, sl st in each of last 3 chs. Cut yarn, leaving approx 6″ sewing length.

Sew berries tog at center edge of Foundation Row (for button). Button napkin ring closed, sew one leaf on each side of closure.

PORTRAIT PILLOWS

designed by Anis Duncan

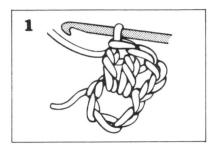

MR. SNOWMAN PILLOW

Here are bright and colorful portraits of favorite winter figures—Mr. Snowman, Santa and Mrs. Santa. They are fun and easy to make from a new version of the traditional granny square. They will make ideal decorations at Christmas, but you'll just hate to pack them away when the holidays are over!

Size

Approx 16″ square

Materials

Worsted weight yarn:
    6 oz green
    2½ oz white
    2 oz black
    3 yds blue
    5 yds red
Aluminum crochet hook size I (or size required for gauge)
16″ square knife-edge pillow form

Gauge

One square = 2½″

Square Instructions

ONE-COLOR SQUARE: Ch 4, join with a sl st to form a ring.

Rnd 1 (wrong side): Ch 3, 2 dc in ring (*Fig 1*); ch 2, (3 dc in ring, ch 2) 3 times; join with a sl st in top of beg ch-3 (*Fig 2*).

Rnd 2: Turn; sk joining st, sl st in next ch st and into

ch-2 sp; ch 3, 2 dc in same sp; * ch 1, work (3 dc, ch 2, 3 dc) all in next ch-2 sp for corner; rep from * twice more; ch 1, 3 dc in beg corner sp (*Fig 3*); ch 2, join with a sl st in top of beg ch-3. Finish off, leaving 8″ sewing length for joining later.

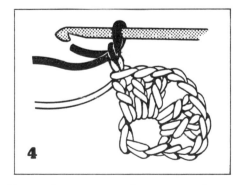

DIAGONAL TWO-COLOR SQUARE: With color A, ch 4, join with a sl st to form a ring.

Rnd 1 (wrong side): Ch 3, 2 dc in ring; ch 2, 3 dc in ring; drop color A (do not cut); with color B, ch 2 (*Fig 4*) continuing with color B, (3 dc in ring, ch 2) twice; join with a sl st in top of beg ch-3 of color A.

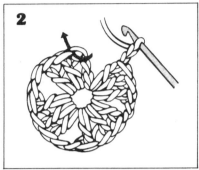

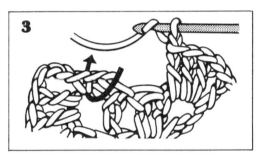

Rnd 2: Turn; sk joining st, sl st in next ch st and into ch-2 sp; ch 3, 2 dc in same sp; ch 1, work (3 dc, ch 2, 3 dc) all in next ch-2 sp for corner; ch 1, 3 dc in

next ch-2 sp; ch 2, drop color B; with color A, work 3 dc in same sp, ch 1; continuing with color A, work (3 dc, ch 2, 3 dc) all in next ch-2 sp, ch 1; work 3 dc in beg corner sp (over 2 sl sts of color B), ch 2; join with a sl st in top of beg ch-3 of color B. Finish off, leaving approx 8″ sewing lengths.

QUANTITIES: Following One-Color Square and Diagonal Two-Color Square instructions, make the following number of squares:

ONE-COLOR SQUARES	DIAGONAL TWO-COLOR SQUARES
	color A / color B
40 green	3 green/white
11 black	1 black/white
17 white	

Assembling Squares

BACK: Use 36 green One-Color Squares to make 6 rows with 6 squares in each row. To join, hold 2 squares with right sides tog, positioned (whenever possible) with sewing length in upper right-hand corner. Carefully matching sts across, beg in ch st at corner and sew with overcast st in **outer lps only** (**Fig 5**), ending in ch st at next corner. Make 6 rows of 6 squares each; then join all 6 rows, being careful to secure each 4-corner junction.

FRONT: Assemble rem squares as shown in (**Fig 6**) and join in same manner as back. When all squares are joined, work the following applique details.

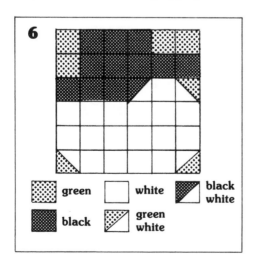

green   white   black white

black   green white

Applique Details

As each detail is made, weave in yarn ends; then use matching yarn and sew to front of pillow (refer to photo for position).

NOSE: With red, ch 3, join with a sl st to form a ring. Ch 3, 11 dc in ring, join with a sl st in top of beg ch-3; finish off. Before sewing to front of pillow, stuff with small amount of yarn scraps.

LEFT EYE: With blue, ch 3, join with a sl st to form a ring.

Row 1 (wrong side): Ch 1, 6 sc in ring.

Row 2: Ch 2, turn; sc in first sc, 2 sc in next sc; 2 hdc in each of next 2 sc, 2 dc in each of last 2 sc; finish off.

RIGHT EYE: With blue, ch 3, join with a sl st to form a ring.

Row 1 (wrong side): Ch 1, 6 sc in ring.

Row 2: Ch 3, turn; dc in first sc, 2 dc in next sc; 2 hdc in each of next 2 sc, 2 sc in each of last 2 sc; finish off.

MOUTH: With 2 strands of red, ch 26, finish off. Sew right side of chain to pillow having wrong side facing you.

PIPE: With black, ch 11.

Row 1 (right side): Sc in **top lp only** of 2nd ch from hook and in each of next 8 chs, 3 sc in last ch. Turn chain slightly clockwise; working on opposite side of chain, sc in each of next 2 chs, sl st in next ch.

Row 2: Ch 1, turn; sc in sl st, sc in each of next 3 sc.

Row 3: Ch 1, turn; sc in each of 4 sc across.

Row 4: Ch 1, turn; 2 sc in first sc, sc in each of rem 3 sc.

Row 5: Ch 1, turn; sk first sc, sc in each of next 3 sc, sl st in last sc. Finish off.

Finishing

Hold front and back of pillow with wrong sides tog; join green with a sl st in ch st at any outer corner; ch 1, sc in same st. Carefully matching sts and seams and working through **inner lps only,** sc in corresponding sts of both pieces around 3 sides. Insert pillow form; then join last edge. Join with a sl st in beg sc; finish off and weave in all yarn ends.

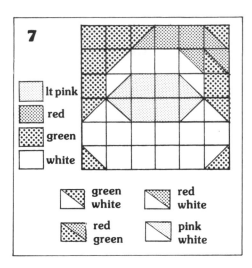

⬚	lt pink
▨	red
▧	green
☐	white

◹ green / white		◹ red / white	
◹ red / green		◹ pink / white	

SANTA PILLOW

Size

Approx 16″ square

Materials

Worsted weight yarn:
- 8 oz red
- 1½ oz green
- 2 oz white
- 1 oz light pink
- 12 yds dark pink
- 6 yds blue

Aluminum crochet hook size I (or size required for gauge)

16″ square knife-edge pillow form

Square Instructions

Following One-Color Square and Diagonal Two-Color Square instructions in Snowman Pillow, make squares as follows:

ONE-COLOR SQUARES	DIAGONAL TWO-COLOR SQUARES
	color A / color B
4 lt pink	5 green / white
38 red	1 red / white
5 green	3 red / green
12 white	4 pink / white

Assembling Squares

BACK: Assemble and join 36 red One-Color Squares in same manner as Snowman Pillow.

FRONT: Assemble rem squares as shown in *Fig 7* and join in same manner as back. When all squares are joined, work the following facial features.

Facial Features

As each feature is made, weave in yarn ends; then use matching yarn and sew to front of pillow (refer to photo for position).

NOSE, LEFT EYE AND RIGHT EYE: Work same as in Snowman Pillow.

LEFT CHEEK: With dk pink, ch 3, join with a sl st to form a ring.

Row 1 (right side): Ch 3, 5 dc in ring.

Row 2: Ch 3, turn; dc in first dc, 2 dc in each of rem 4 dc, 2 dc in top of ch-3.

Row 3: TURN, sk first dc, sl st in next dc; ch 1, hdc in next dc; 2 dc in each of next 8 dc, 2 dc in top of ch-3; finish off.

RIGHT CHEEK: With dk pink, ch 3, join with a sl st to form a ring.

Row 1 (right side): Ch 3, 5 dc in ring.

Row 2: Ch 3, turn; dc in first dc, 2 dc in each of rem 4 dc, 2 dc in top of ch-3.

Row 3: Ch 3, turn; sk first dc, dc in next dc; 2 dc in each of next 8 dc, hdc in next dc, sc in top of ch-3; finish off.

Finishing

Hold front and back of pillow with wrong sides tog; join red with a sl st at any outer corner; ch 1, sc in same st. Carefully matching sts and seams and working through **inner lps only,** sc in corresponding sts of both pieces around 3 sides. Insert pillow form; then join last edge. Join with a sl st in beg sc; finish off and weave in all yarn ends. With white, make 2″ diameter pompon *(see page 11)* and sew to pillow as shown in photo.

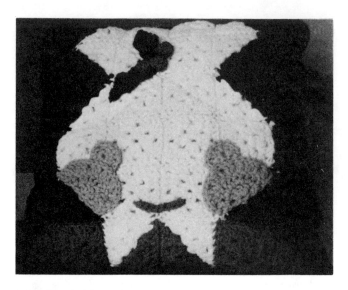

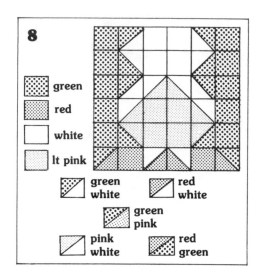

MRS. SANTA PILLOW

Size

Approx 16″ square

Materials

Worsted weight yarn:
    8 oz green
    1 oz red
    1½ oz white
    1 oz light pink
    12 yds dark pink
    6 yds blue
Aluminum crochet hook size I (or size required for gauge)
16″ square knife-edge pillow form

Gauge

One square = 2½″

Square Instructions

Following One-Color Square and Diagonal Two-Color Square instructions in Santa Pillow, make squares as follows:

ONE-COLOR SQUARES	DIAGONAL TWO-COLOR SQUARES
	color A / color B
46 green	6 green/white
2 red	2 red/white
4 white	2 green/pink
4 lt pink	4 pink/white
	2 red/green

Assembling Squares

BACK: Assemble and join 36 green One-Color Squares in same manner as Snowman Pillow.

FRONT: Assemble rem squares as shown in *Fig 8* and join in same manner as back. When all squares are joined, work the following applique details.

Applique Details

As each detail is made, weave in yarn ends; then use matching yarn and sew to front of pillow (refer to photo for position).

LEFT EYE, RIGHT EYE, LEFT CHEEK AND RIGHT CHEEK: Work same as in Santa Pillow.

MOUTH: With 2 strands of red, ch 8, finish off. Sew right side of chain to pillow having wrong side facing you.

LEAVES (make 2): With green, ch 11. Working **in top lp only** of each ch across: sl st in 2nd ch from hook, sc in next ch, hdc in next ch, † dc in next ch, ch 3, sl st in first ch of ch-3 just made †; sc in next ch, hdc in next ch; rep from † to † once; sc in next ch, sl st in next ch, 3 sl sts in last ch. Turn piece slightly and continue by working on opposite side of starting ch: sl st in first ch, sc in next ch; rep from † to † once; sc in next ch, hdc in next ch; rep from † to † once; sc in next ch, sl st in each of last 3 chs. Finish off, leaving 6″ sewing length.

BERRIES (make 3): With red, ch 2.

Rnd 1: Work 6 sc in 2nd ch from hook.

Rnds 2 and 3: Sc in each sc around. Finish off, leaving 6″ end. Thread into tapestry needle and weave through sts of last rnd; draw up tightly and fasten securely.

Finishing

Use green and join front and back of pillow in same manner as Santa Pillow.

BRAIDED CHRISTMAS WREATH

designed by Mary Thomas

Size
Approx 12″ diameter

Materials
Worsted weight yarn:
    3 oz lt green
    6 oz dk green
    ¼ oz red
Aluminum crochet hooks sizes F and J (or size
    required for gauge)
1½ yds 2″ red grosgrain ribbon
Polyester filling for stuffing.

Gauge
With 2 strands of yarn and larger size hook in sc,
5 sts = 2″; 3 rnds = 1″

Instructions
(Make one lt green tubular piece and 2 dark green.)
With 2 strands of yarn and larger size hook, ch 12,
join with a sl st in beg ch to form ring. [*NOTE:
Throughout pattern, do not join rnds; all rnds are
worked on right side.*]

Rnd 1: Ch 1, sc in same ch as joining and in each
rem ch around = 12 sc.

Rnd 2: Sc **in back lp only** of each sc around.
Lightly stuffing piece as you work, rep Rnd 2 until
piece measures approx 44″. Finish off, leaving 10″
sewing length.

BERRIES (make 9)

Instructions
With single strand of red and smaller size hook,
ch. 2.

Rnd 1: Work 6 sc in 2nd ch from hook.

Rnds 2 and 3: Sc in each sc around. Cut yarn,
leaving approx 6″ end; thread into tapestry needle.
Weave through sts of last rnd and draw up tightly;
fasten securely, leaving yarn end for sewing.

Finishing
Braid tubular pieces and form a wreath; sew matching ends tog. Make ribbon bow and attach to wreath
over joining of tubular pieces. Sew berries in clusters
of 3 evenly spaced around wreath.

FILET WALL HANGINGS

These magnificent designs revive the lovely old art of filet crochet. If you've been afraid to try filet, Mary Thomas' new method of instructions makes it a breeze. These are not difficult projects, but they do require a good bit of time to complete... time worth investing in pieces sure to become family heirlooms.

SPECIAL FILET INSTRUCTIONS

Filet design is worked from a chart of squares. On each odd-numbered row (right side of work), work chart from right to left; on each even-numbered row (wrong side of work), work chart from left to right.

ON EACH ROW OF CHART: Work each vertical line as one dc (Fig 1). At beg of row, work the first vertical line as ch 3 (counts as one dc). Each following vertical line (dc) is worked in dc (vertical line) in row below, ending by working last vertical line (dc) in top of ch-3 in row below.

Work each open (non-shaded) sp between 2 vertical lines (dcs) as one ch (Fig 2). For an open sp at beg or row, beg with ch 3 for first vertical line, then ch one more for first open sp for a total of 4 chs (Fig 2). For each open sp, you will sk in row below either a ch-1 sp (open sp) or one dc (filled-in sp).

Work each filled-in (shaded) sp between 2 vertical lines (dcs) as one dc (Fig 3). For each filled-in sp, you will work in row below either into ch-1 sp (open sp) or in dc (filled-in sp).

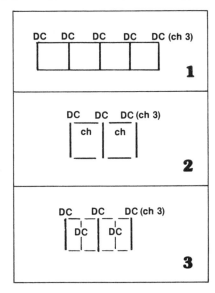

CHRISTMAS ANGEL WALL HANGING

Size

Approx 18" wide x 24" long

Materials

American Thread GIANT Crochet Thread:
    550 yds White
Size 5 steel crochet hook (or size required for gauge)
20" dowel rod, ¼" diameter

Gauge

In dc, 8 sts = 1"; 4 rows = 1"

Instructions

Ch 165 loosely. (*NOTE: Ch-3 counts as one dc throughout patt.*)

Row 1: Dc in 4th ch from hook and in each of next 11 chs; * ch 2, sk 2 chs, dc in each of next 7 chs; rep from * across, ending last rep by working dc in each of last 13 chs.

Row 2: Ch 3, turn; dc in each of next 6 dc, (ch 2, sk 2 dc, dc in next dc) twice; * 2 dc in ch-2 sp, dc in next dc, (ch 2, sk 2 dc, dc in next dc) twice; rep from * across, ending by working dc in each of next 5 dc, dc, dc in top of Tch.

Now refer to chart in **Fig 4.** You have just com-

Row 3
Row 1

39

pleted the first 2 rows; compare your work to the chart. From this point on, you will be working from the chart. Beg with Row 3 of chart and work until all rows of chart have been completed. Do not finish off.

TOP EDGING: Row 1: Ch 1, turn; sc in each dc and 2 sc in each ch-2 sp across, ending by working sc in top of Tch = 163 sc.

Row 2: Ch 10, turn; sk next sc, * sc in each of next 3 sc; ch 10, sk next sc; rep from * across, ending by working sc in last sc.

Finishing

Place hanging on a flat padded surface covered with a clean white sheet. Keeping edges straight, insert rust-proof pins in sts around edges. Then spray with a commercial spray starch until wet. Let dry thoroughly before removing pins. Insert dowel rod through ch-10 lps at top of hanging.

NATIVITY SCENE WALL HANGING

designed by Anis Duncan

Size

Approx 23″ wide x 36″ long

Materials

Bedspread weight crochet cotton:
    Five 250-yd balls white
Steel crochet hook size 5 (or size required for gauge)
24″ dowel rod, ¼″ diamater

Gauge

In dc, 8 sts = 1″; 4 rows = 1″

Instructions

Ch 185 loosely. *(NOTE: Ch-3 counts as one dc throughout patt.)*

Row 1 (right side): Dc in 4th ch from hook and in each rem ch across = 183 dc (counting ch-3).

Row 2: Ch 3, turn; sk first dc, dc in each of next 2 dc; ch 1 loosely, sk one dc, dc in next dc; * ch 1 loosely, sk one dc, dc in each of next 3 dc; rep from * to last 6 dc; (ch 1 loosely, sk one dc, dc in next dc) twice; dc in next dc, dc in top of ch-3.

Row 3: Ch 3, turn; sk first dc, dc in each of next 2 dc; (ch 1 loosely, sk ch-1 sp, dc in next dc) twice; * ch 1 loosely, sk one dc, dc in next dc; ch 1 loosely, sk ch-1 sp, dc in next dc; rep from * to last ch-1 sp; ch 1 loosely, sk last ch-1 sp, dc in each of next 2 dc, dc in top of ch-3.

Now refer to chart in *Fig 5*. You have just completed the first 3 rows; compare your work to the chart. From this point on, you will work only from the chart. *(NOTE: Remember to work each ch-1 loosely.)* Beg with Row 4 of chart and work through last row of chart. At end of last row, do not finish off.

TOP EDGING: Row 1: Ch 1, turn; sc in each dc across, ending sc in top of ch-3 = 183 sc.

Row 2: Ch 10, turn; sk first 2 sc, * sc in each of next 3 sc, ch 10, sk one sc; rep from * to last sc, sc in last sc. Finish off, weave in all ends.

5

Row 2 ——————

— Row 3
— Row 1

START

Finishing

Place hanging on a flat padded surface covered with a clean white sheet. Keeping edges straight, insert rust-proof pins in sts around edges. Then spray with a commercial spray starch until wet. Let dry thoroughly before removing pins. Insert dowel rod through ch-10 lps at top of hanging.

"Not a creature was stirring..."

. . . not even the Christmas mouse because he's crocheted from the tip of his hat to his Santa bag. The other Christmas creatures are crocheted and ready to add to the holiday festivities.

CHRISTMAS PUPPY

designed by Sue Penrod

A charming crocheted puppy to use as a holiday decoration or special Christmas toy. Dressed in his red scarf and winter hat, he arrives at your festivities carrying his own present.

Size

Approx 8″ tall

Materials

Worsted weight yarn:
    3 oz tan
    ½ oz red
    12 yds green
    4 yds black
Size H aluminum crochet hook (or size required for gauge)
Polyester fiber (for stuffing)
Small felt pieces in black and white
Tracing paper and pencil
White craft glue
Size 16 tapestry needle

Gauge

In sc, 7sts = 2″

Instructions

NOTE: Throughout patt, unless otherwise specified, do not join rnds. Use a small safety pin or piece of yarn in contrasting color and mark first st of rnd; move marker at beg of each rnd. This will not be mentioned again in instructions.

HEAD AND BODY: Beg at top of head, with tan, ch 4; join with a sl st to form a ring.

Rnd 1: Work 2 sc in each ch around = 8 sc.

Rnd 2: Working in back lp (lp away from you—*Fig 1*)of each sc (now and throughout head and body), 2 sc in each sc around = 16 sc.

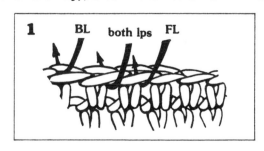

43

Rnd 3: Rep Rnd 2 = 32 sc.

Rnd 4 through 9: Sc in each sc around.

Rnd 10: * Sc in each of next 2 sc, sk one sc, sc in next sc; rep from * around = 24 sc.

Rnd 11: Sc in each sc around.

Rnd 12: Rep Rnd 10 = 18 sc. Before working next rnd, lightly stuff and shape head. [NOTE: Stuffing should not be visible through sts.]

Rnd 13: Sc in each of next 2 sc; * sk one sc, sc in each of next 3 sc; rep from * around = 14 sc.

Rnd 14: Sc in each sc around. Head is now completed; continue with body as follows.

Rnd 15: Work 2 sc in each sc around = 28 sc.

Rnd 16: Sc in each sc around.

Rnd 17 (marking rnd): Sc in each of next 7 sc; * sc in next sc and mark this st (use marker different from beg of rnd) for joining front leg later *; sc in each of next 12 sc; rep from * to * once, sc in each of rem 7 sc.

Rnds 18 through 24: Sc in each sc around.

Rnd 25: * Sc in each of next 2 sc, 2 sc in next sc; rep from * to last sc, sc in last sc = 37 sc.

Rnds 26 through 29: Sc in each sc around.

Rnd 30 (marking rnd): (NOTE: In this rnd, 4 sts are marked for sewing hind legs to body later.) Sc in next sc, (sk one sc, sc in each of next 3 sc) twice; mark last sc worked; sk one sc, sc in each of next 3 sc; sk one sc, sc in each of next 2 sc; mark last sc worked; sc in next sc, sk one sc, sc in each of next 3 sc; sk one sc, sc in next sc and mark this st; sc in each of next 2 sc, sk one sc, sc in each of next 3 sc; mark last sc worked; (sk one sc, sc in each of next 3 sc) twice = 28 sc.

Rnd 31: * Sc in each of next 2 sc, sk one sc, sc in next sc; rep from * around = 21 sc. Before working next rnd, lightly stuff and shape body.

Rnd 32: Sc in next sc; * sk one sc, sc in each of next 3 sc; rep from * around = 16 sc.

Rnd 33: Rep Rnd 31 = 12 sc. Cut yarn, leaving approx 8″ end. Thread into tapestry needle; weave through sts of last rnd. Draw up tightly and fasten securely.

FRONT LEGS (worked in one piece): With tan, leave approx 12″ end for sewing leg to body later, ch 12; join with a sl st to form a ring.

Rnd 1: Sc in each ch around = 12 sc.

Rnds 2 through 6: Working in both lps of each sc (now and throughout legs), sc in each sc around.

Rnd 7: * Sc in each of next 2 sc, 2 sc in next sc; rep from * around = 16 sc.

Rnds 8 and 9: Sc in each sc around.

Rnd 10: * Sc in next sc, sk one sc; rep from * around = 8 sc.

Rnd 11: Rep Rnd 10 = 4 sc. One leg is now completed; continue with other leg as follows.

Rnd 12: Work 2 sc in each sc around = 8 sc.

Rnd 13: Rep Rnd 12 = 16 sc.

Rnds 14 and 15: Sc in each sc around.

Rnd 16: * Sc in each of next 2 sc, sk one sc, sc in next sc; rep from * around = 12 sc.

Rnds 17 through 22: Sc in each sc around. At end of Rnd 22, join with a sl st in beg sc. Cut yarn, leaving approx 12″ sewing length. Lightly stuff and shape leg just made. Thread sewing length into tapestry needle and sew edge closed, carefully matching corresponding 6 sc across. Then sew this edge to side of body below marker. Stuff and sew other leg to body in same manner, having 14 sc free across back.

HIND LEGS (make 2): With tan, leave approx 12″ end for sewing leg to body later, ch 12; join with a sl st to form a ring.

Rnd 1: Sc in each ch around = 12 sc.

Rnd 2: Working in both lps of each sc (now and throughout leg), 2 sc in each sc around = 24 sc.

Rnds 3 and 4: Sc in each sc around.

Rnd 5: * Sl st in next st, sk one st; rep from * around = 12 sl sts.

Rnd 6: Rep Rnd 5 = 6 sl sts. Cut yarn, leaving approx 6″ end. Thread into tapestry needle; weave through sts of last rnd. Draw up tightly and fasten securely on inside. Lightly stuff; sew edge closed, carefully matching corresponding 6 sc across. Then sew this edge to lower front of body between one set of markers.

TAIL: With tan, ch 2.

Rnd 1: Work 3 sc in 2nd ch from hook.

Rnd 2: Working in both lps of each sc (now and throughout tail), 2 sc in each sc around = 6 sc.

Rnds 3 and 4: Sc in each sc around. Cut yarn, leaving approx 8″ sewing length. Thread into tapestry needle; sew edge of last rnd closed and attach to lower center back of body.

MUZZLE: With tan, make two 1″ diameter pompons (see page 11). Attach pompons side by side to lower center front of head. For nose, make ½″ diameter black pompon and attach between and at top of other pompons.

HAT: With red, ch 4, join with a sl st to form a ring.

Rnd 1: Work 2 sc in each ch around = 8 sc.

Rnd 2: Working in back lp of each sc (now and throughout hat), 2 sc in each sc around = 16 sc.

Rnd 3: Rep Rnd 2 = 32 sc.

Rnd 4: Sc in each of next 10 sc; ch 2, sk 2 sc (opening for ear), sc in each of next 8 sc; ch 2, sk 2 sc (opening for other ear), sc in each of rem 10 sc.

Rnd 5: Sc in each sc and in each ch around = 32 sc.

Rnds 6 through 11: Sc in each sc around. At end of Rnd 11, join with a sl st in beg sc. Finish off; weave in ends. Roll up last 2 rnds for brim. Place hat on top of head, having ear openings toward front.

EARS (make 2): With tan, ch 4. **Working under 2 top threads of each ch,** work (hdc, dc, tr) in 2nd ch from hook, 2 tr in next ch, work (dc, hdc, sc) in last ch. Join with a sl st in beg hdc, pushing wrong side of sts toward outside of ear. Cut yarn, leaving approx 8″ sewing length. Thread into tapestry needle; sew ear to head through opening in hat.

PACKAGE: Beg at top, with green, ch 4; join with a sl st to form a ring.

Rnd 1: Work 2 sc in each ch around = 8 sc.

Rnd 2: Working in back lp of each sc (now and throughout package), 2 sc in each sc around = 16 sc.

Rnds 3 through 9: Sc in each sc around. At end of Rnd 9, lightly stuff and shape package.

Rnd 10: * Sk one sc, sl st in next sc; rep from * around = 8 sl sts. Cut yarn, leaving approx 6″ end. Thread into tapestry needle; weave through sts of last rnd. Draw up tightly and fasten securely. For trim, use red and make a chain to measure approx 26″ long; finish off and weave in ends. With smooth side of chain facing package, wrap chain around each side of package and tie into a bow at top. Place package in front legs.

SCARF: With red, ch 60. Work dc in 4th ch from hook and in each rem ch across. Finish off; weave in ends. Tie scarf around neck, having ends at side of puppy.

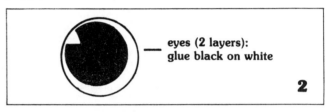
eyes (2 layers): glue black on white

2

EYES: Trace outlines in *Fig 2* on paper. Cut outlines and use as patterns on felt as indicated. With glue, attach felt pieces as shown in photo.

SNOWLADY AND SNOWMAN

designed by Sue Penrod

This popular pair, adorned in their Christmas finery, will make delightful holiday decorations. If you stuff their bases (plastic tubs) with popcorn kernels, you've made a set of rattle toys just the perfect size for little hands to hold and shake. What could be more fun for that special Christmas baby!

Size

Approx 8½" tall

Materials

Worsted weight yarn:
   4 oz white
   ½ oz green
   ½ oz black
   20 yds red
Size J aluminum crochet hook (or size required for gauge)
White plastic bowls with lid (4-oz non-dairy whipped topping size) filled with ½ cup of popcorn kernels (for rattle)
Polyester fiber (for stuffing)
Small felt pieces in black and red
Tracing paper and pencil
White craft glue
Size 16 tapestry needle

Gauge

In sc, 3 sts = 1"

SNOWLADY

Instructions

NOTE: Throughout patt, unless otherwise specified, do not join rnds. Use a small safety pin or piece of yarn in contrasting color and mark first st of rnd; move marker at beg of each rnd. This will not be mentioned again in instructions.

BODY AND HEAD: Beg at bottom of body, with white, ch 4; join with a sl st to form a ring.

Rnd 1: Work 2 sc in each ch around = 8 sc.

Rnd 2: Working in back lp (lp away from you—*Fig 1*) of each sc (now and throughout body and head), 2 sc in each sc around = 16 sc.

Rnd 3: Rep Rnd 2 = 32 sc.

Rnd 4: Sc in each of next 2 sc; * 2 sc in next sc, sc in each of next 2 sc; rep from * around = 42 sc.

Rnds 5 through 18: Sc in each sc around. At end

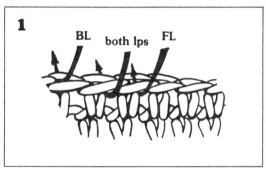

of Rnd 18, insert bowl (filled with popcorn kernels, if rattle is desired,) into body, with lid at top.

Rnd 19: Sc in each of next 2 sc; * sk one sc, sc in each of next 3 sc; rep from * around = 32 sc.

Rnd 20: Sc in each of next 2 sc; * sk one sc, sc in each of next 2 sc; rep from * around = 22 sc. Before working next rnd, stuff body lightly. [*NOTE: Stuffing should not be visible through sts.*]

Rnd 21: * Sc in next sc, sk one sc, rep from * around = 11 sc. Body is now completed; continue with head as follows.

Rnd 22: Work 2 sc in each sc around = 22 sc.

Rnd 23: * Sc in next sc, 2 sc in next sc; rep from * around = 33 sc.

Rnds 24 through 29: Sc in each sc around.

Rnd 30: Sc in next sc; * sk one sc, sc in each of next 3 sc; rep from * around = 25 sc.

Rnd 31: Sc in next sc; * sk one sc, sc in each of next 2 sc; rep from * around = 17 sc. Before working next rnd, stuff head lightly.

Rnd 32: Sl st in next sc; * sk one sc, sl st in next sc; rep from * around = 9 sl sts. Cut yarn, leaving approx 8″ end. Thread into tapestry needle; weave through sts of last rnd. Draw up lightly and fasten securely.

ARMS (*make 2*): With white, leave approx 12″ end for sewing arm to body later, ch 15; join with a sl st to form a ring.

Rnd 1: Sc in each ch around = 15 sc.

Rnd 2: Working in both lps of each sc (now and throughout arm), 2 sc in each sc around = 30 sc.

Rnd 3: Sc in each sc around.

Rnd 4: * Sc in next sc, sk one sc, sc in next sc; rep from * around = 20 sc.

Rnd 5: * Sk one sc, sc in next sc; rep from * around = 10 sc.

Rnd 6: * Sk one sc, sl st in next sc; rep from * around = 5 sl sts. Cut yarn, leaving approx 6″ end. Thread into tapestry needle; weave through sts of last rnd. Draw up tightly and fasten securely on inside. Stuff arm lightly; then sew open circular edge to side of body, approx 2 rnds below neck.

BONNET: With green, ch 4, join with a sl st to form a ring.

Rnd 1: Work 2 sc in each ch around = 8 sc.

Rnd 2: Working in back lp of each sc (now and throughout bonnet), 2 sc in each sc around = 16 sc.

Rnd 3: Rep Rnd 2 = 32 sc.

Rnds 4 through 10: Sc in each sc around.

Rnd 11 (brim and tie): Tr (triple crochet) in next sc. * Work 2 tr in next sc, tr in next sc; rep from * 11 times more (7 sc rem); sc in both lps of next sc, continue with same yarn and make a chain to measure approx 16″ long (for tie); sk next 5 sc, join with a sl st in both lps of last sc, being careful not to twist chain. Finish off; weave in ends. Place bonnet on head and tie bow at front of neck.

APRON: With red, ch 57.

Row 1 (right side): Sc in 2nd ch from hook, hdc in each of next 2 chs, dc in each of next 3 chs; 2 tr in each of next 6 chs, dc in each of next 3 chs; hdc in each of next 2 chs, sl st in next ch (rem chs are left unworked for one tie).

Row 2: Ch 3, turn; **working in both lps of each st,** sl st in first hdc, * ch 3, sk one st, sl st in next st; rep from * across. Continuing with same yarn, ch 38 (for other tie). Finish off; knot and trim end of each tie. Place apron around body just below arms and tie bow at center back.

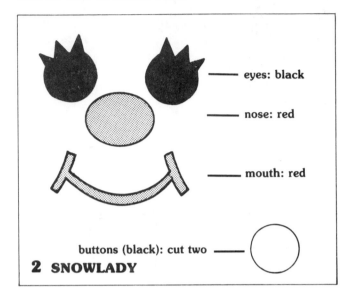

2 SNOWLADY

— eyes: black

— nose: red

— mouth: red

buttons (black): cut two ——

Finishing

For facial features and buttons, trace outlines in *Fig 2* on paper. Cut outlines and use as patterns on felt as indicated. With glue, attach felt pieces as shown in photo.

SNOWMAN
Instructions

NOTE: Throughout patt, unless otherwise specified, do not join rnds. Use a small safety pin or piece of yarn in contrasting color and mark first st of rnd; move marker at beg of each rnd. This will not be mentioned again in instructions.

BODY, HEAD AND ARMS: Work same as Snowlady.

HAT: With black, ch 4, join with a sl st to form a ring.

Rnd 1: Work 2 sc in each ch around = 8 sc.

Rnd 2: Working in back lp of each sc (now and throughout hat), 2 sc in each sc around = 16 sc.

Rnd 3: * Sc in next sc, 2 sc in next sc; rep from * around = 24 sc.

Rnds 4 through 11: Sc in each sc around.

Rnd 12 (brim): Sl st in next sc, ch 3, 2 dc in next sc; * dc in next sc, 2 dc in next sc; rep from * around, join with a sl st in top of beg ch-3. Cut yarn, leaving approx 12″ sewing length. Thread into tapestry needle and sew hat in place on top of head as shown in photo.

SCARF: With red, ch 60. Hdc in 3rd ch from hook and in each rem ch across. Finish off; weave in ends. Tie scarf around neck, having ends at center front.

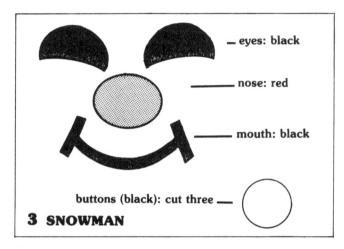

eyes: black

nose: red

mouth: black

buttons (black): cut three

3 SNOWMAN

Finishing

For facial features and buttons, trace outlines in *Fig 3* on paper. Cut outlines and use as patterns on felt as indicated. With glue, attach felt pieces as shown in photo.

SANTA MOUSE

If you're a collector of Mouseiana, here's the perfect addition. Our crocheted mouse is all dressed for Christmas; in fact, he's making believe he's Santa Claus, complete with his bag of gifts for all the good little mice girls and boys.

Size

Approx 10″ tall

Materials

Worsted weight yarn:
   2 oz gray
   2 oz red
   ½ oz white
   ½ oz gold
   10 yds black
   2 yds green
Size H aluminum crochet hook (or size required for gauge)
3 Gold ¼″ jingle bells (for buttons)
Black floral wire: 12″ length (for whiskers)
Small felt pieces in black and white
Tracing paper and pencil
White craft glue
Polyester fiber (for stuffing)
Size 16 tapestry needle

NOTE: For whiskers, black carpet thread (stiffened with coating of glue) may be substituted for floral wire.

Gauge

In sc, 7 sts = 2″

Instructions

BODY: Beg at bottom, with gray, ch 2.

Rnd 1: Work 6 sc in 2nd ch from hook. Use small safety pin or piece of yarn in contrasting color and mark last st for end of rnd; move marker at end of each rnd. Do not join rnds.

Rnd 2: Work 2 sc in each sc around = 12 sc.

Rnd 3: * Sc in next sc, 2 sc in next sc; rep from * around = 18 sc.

Rnd 4: Rep Rnd 3 = 27 sc.

Rnd 5: * Sc in each of next 2 sc, 2 sc in next sc; rep from * around = 36 sc.

Rnds 6 through 11: Sc in each sc around.

Rnd 12: * Work 2 sc in next sc, sc in each of next 3 sc; rep from * around = 45 sc.

Rnds 13, 14 and 15: Sc in each sc around. At end of Rnd 15, finish off gray; join red.

Rnds 16 and 17: Continuing with red jacket, sc in each sc around.

Rnd 18: * Sc in each of next 3 sc, dec over next 2 sc. [**To Dec: Draw up a lp in each of next 2 sc, YO and draw through all 3 lps on hook = dec made**]; rep from * around = 36 sc.

Rnds 19 through 23: Sc in each sc around.

Rnd 24: * Sc in each of next 4 sc, dec over next 2 sc; rep from * around = 30 sc. Before working next rnd, stuff body firmly.

Rnd 25: Sc in each sc around.

Rnd 26: * Sc in each of next 3 sc, dec over next 2 sc; rep from * around = 24 sc.

Rnd 27: Sc in each sc around.

Rnd 28: * Sc in each of next 2 sc, dec over next 2 sc; rep from * around = 18 sc.

Rnd 29: Sc in each sc around.

Rnd 30: * Sc in next sc, dec over next 2 sc; rep from * around = 12 sc.

Rnds 31 and 32: Sc in each sc around. At end of Rnd 32, cut yarn, leaving approx 12″ sewing length. Finish stuffing body. Set aside, leaving neck open.

JACKET TRIM: With white, ch 45; join with a sl st to form a ring, being careful not to twist chain.

Rnd 1: Ch 1, sc in each ch around; join with a sl st in beg sc = 45 sc.

Rnd 2: Ch 1, sc in same st as joining and in each rem sc around; join with a sl st in beg sc = 45 sc.

Rnd 3: Rep Rnd 2. Finish off; weave in ends. With last rnd worked at top, slip trim over neck and then down around middle of body where colors were changed. Tack in place, if desired.

COLLAR: With white, ch 18, join with a sl st to form a ring. Rep Rnds 1 and 2 of Jacket Trim, having 18 sc in each rnd. Finish off; weave in ends. With the last rnd worked at bottom, slip collar around neck of body. Tack in place, if desired.

HEAD: Beg at tip of nose, with gray, ch 2.

Rnd 1: Work 4 sc in 2nd ch from hook. As before, mark last of rnd; do not join rnds.

Rnd 2: Work 2 sc in each sc around = 8 sc.

Rnd 3: Sc in each sc around.

Rnd 4: * Sc in next sc, 2 sc in next sc; rep from * around = 12 sc.

Rnds 5 through 8: Rep Rnds 3 and 4, twice. At end of Rnd 6, you should have 18 sc; and at end of Rnd 8, you should have 27 sc.

Rnds 9 through 14: Sc in each sc around.

Rnd 15: * Sc in next sc, dec over next 2 sc; rep from * around = 18 sc.

Rnd 16: Sc in each sc around.

Rnd 17: * Dec over next 2 sc; rep from * around = 9 sc. Cut yarn, leaving approx 8″ sewing length. Stuff head firmly, using pencil to push stuffing down into tip of nose. Thread sewing length into tapestry needle; weave through sts of last rnd. Draw up tightly and fasten securely. Now attach head to body as follows. Thread sewing length left on body (at neck) into tapestry needle. Place head on neck of body, aligning 4th rnd from closure of head at back of neck. Sew in place, having nose protruding over and slightly down over body.

EARS (make 2): Beg at bottom edge of outer ear, with gray (leave approx 16″ sewing length), ch 7.

Row 1: Sc in 2nd ch from hook and in each rem ch across = 6 sc.

Row 2: Ch 1, turn; 2 sc in first sc, sc in each of next 4 sc, 2 sc in last sc = 8 sc.

Rows 3 and 4: Ch 1, turn; sc in each sc across.

Row 5: Ch 1, turn; dec over first 2 sc, sc in each sc across to last 2 sc; dec over last 2 sc = 6 sc.

Row 6: Rep Row 5 = 4 sc.

Row 7: Ch 1, turn; (dec over 2 sts) twice = 2 sc. Cut gray, leaving approx 2″ end for weaving in later.

Row 8: With white (for inner ear), ch 1, turn; work 2 sc in each sc = 4 sc.

Row 9: Ch 1, turn; 2 sc in first sc, sc in each of next 2 sc, 2 sc in last sc = 6 sc.

Rows 10, 11 and 12: Rep Rows 3, 4 and 5. At end of Row 12, you should have 4 sc. Finish off; weave in end and 2″ gray end (at end of Row 7). Keeping last row worked to outside of ear, fold piece over at color change. Thread beginning gray sewing length into tapestry needle. Weave bottom and side edges of outer and inner ear tog, cupping ear forward. Position ear on top of head (at back), leaving 3 center sc free between ears; sew in place.

HAT: Beg at cuff, with white, ch 24; join with a sl st to form a ring, being careful not to twist chain. Rep Rnds 1 and 2 of Jacket Trim, having 24 sc in each rnd. Finish off; weave in ends. Turn cuff inside out. With wrong side of sts facing you and foundation chain edge across top, join red with a sl st in unused lp of any st of foundation chain.

Rnd 1: Ch 1, sc in same st as joining and in each rem st around = 24 sc. Mark last st of rnd (as before); do not join rnds.

Rnds 2, 3 and 4: Sc in each sc around.

Rnd 5: * Sc in each of next 4 sc, dec over next 2 sc; rep from * around = 20 sc.

Rnd 6: Sc in each sc around.

Rnd 7: * Sc in each of next 3 sc, dec over next 2 sc; rep from * around = 16 sc.

Rnds 8 and 9: Sc in each sc around.

Rnd 10: * Sc in each of next 2 sc, dec over next 2 sc; rep from * around = 12 sc.

Rnds 11, 12 and 13: Sc in each sc around.

Rnd 14: Rep Rnd 10 = 9 sc.

Rnds 15 through 18: Sc in each sc around.

Rnd 19: * Sc in next sc, dec over next 2 sc; rep from * around = 6 sc.

Rnds 20 through 24: Sc in each sc around. At end of Rnd 24, cut yarn leaving approx 6″ end. Thread into tapestry needle; weave through sts of last rnd. Draw up tightly and fasten securely. Make 1″ diameter white pompon (see page 11) and attach to tip of hat. Fold up white cuff. Bend hat as shown in photo and tack into place. Place on head over either ear.

SLEEVE AND MITTEN (make 2): With red (leave approx 12″ sewing length), ch 12; join with a sl st to form a ring.

Rnd 1: Sc in each ch around = 12 sc. Mark last st of rnd (as before); do not join rnds.

Rnds 2 through 5: Sc in each sc around.

Rnd 6: (Dec over next 2 sc) twice, sc in each rem sc around = 10 sc.

Rnds 7, 8 and 9: Sc in each sc around.

Rnd 10: Dec over next 2 sc, sc in each rem sc around = 9 sc.

Rnds 11 and 12: Sc in each sc around.

Rnd 13: Rep Rnd 10 = 8 sc.

Rnd 14: Rep Rnd 10 = 7 sc. Finish off red; join black for mitten.

Rnds 15, 16 and 17: Sc in each sc around. At end of Rnd 17, cut yarn, leaving approx 6″ end. Thread into tapestry needle; weave through sts of last rnd. Draw up tightly and fasten securely. Stuff and shape sleeve and mitten, bending sleeve slightly at elbow. Thread beginning red sewing length into tapestry needle. Sew open edge of sleeve tog, carefully matching 6 corresponding sc across. Then sew this edge to side of mouse in second rnd below white collar.

SLEEVE CUFF (make 2): With white, ch 8, join with a sl st to form a ring. Rep Rnds 1 and 2 of Jacket Trim, having 8 sc in each rnd. Finish off; weave in ends. With last rnd worked at top, slip cuff over mitten and position around end of sleeve where colors were changed. Tack in place, if desired.

TAIL: With gray, make a chain to measure approx 14" long; then work sl st in 2nd ch from hook and in each rem ch across. Cut yarn, leaving approx 4" sewing length. Thread into tapestry needle and sew tail to body at lower center of back.

Bow: With green, make a chain to measure approx 12" long; finish off. Knot and trim each end of chain. Tie chain into a bow around tail, approx 1" from end.

SANTA'S PACK: With gold, work same as Body through Rnd 11.

Rnds 12 through 16: Sc in each sc around.

Rnd 17 (beading rnd): Sl st in next sc, ch 3; dc in each rem sc around, join with a sl st in top of beg ch-3.

Rnd 18: Ch 1, sc in same st as joining and in each rem st around; join with a sl st in beg sc.

Rnd 19: Rep Rnd 18. Finish off; weave in ends.

Drawstring: With black, make a chain to measure approx 15" long; finish off. Weave through sts of Beading Rnd, beg and ending at beg of rnd. Knot both ends of drawstring tog; trim ends. Place Christmas candy or small toy inside of pack; pull drawstring slightly closed and place over either arm.

Finishing

Buttons: With sewing thread, attach 3 jingle bells evenly spaced down front center of jacket.

Nose: With gray, make ¼" diameter pompon and attach to head at tip of nose.

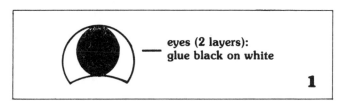

eyes (2 layers):
glue black on white

1

Eyes: Trace outlines in *Fig 1* on paper. Cut outlines and use as patterns on felt as indicated. With glue, attach felt pieces as shown in photo.

Whiskers: Cut floral wire into 3 equal lengths (each approx 4" long). Refer to photo for position and pull each length through end of nose with crochet hook. Dab the ends of each wire with glue to prevent fraying.

SNOWMAN

designed by Winnie Ardito

Our chubby snowman will delight children and adults alike. Stand him near the front door to welcome guests, or on the hearth (he won't melt!); or make him a holiday table centerpiece.

Size

Approx 18" tall with hat

Materials

American Thread Dawn Sayelle Knitting Worsted Size Yarn:
   8 oz White
   3 oz Black
   2 oz Flame
   ¼ oz each of Hot Orange and Golf Green
Sizes G and I aluminum crochet hooks (or size required for gauge)
Polyester fiber (approx 2 lbs) for stuffing
Heavy cardboard circular piece (8" diameter) for base
NOTE: Smaller size hook is used only for holly decoration on hat.

Gauge

With larger size hook in sc, 7 sts = 2"

Instructions:

NOTE: Throughout patt, unless otherwise specified, do not join rnds. Use a small safety pin or piece of yarn in contrasting color and mark first st of rnd; move marker at beg of each rnd. When instructions say to "work even", work sc in each st for specified number of rnds without increasing or decreasing.

Beg at bottom, with larger size hook and White, ch 2.

Rnd 1: Work 6 sc in 2nd ch from hook on inside; wrong side of sts will be facing outside of snowman.

Rnd 2: * Work 2 sc in next sc (inc made); rep from * 5 times more = 12 sc.

Rnd 3: * Inc, sc in next sc; rep from * around = 18 sc.

Rnd 4: Rep Rnd 3 = 27 sc.

Rnd 5: * Inc, sc in each of next 2 sc; rep from * around = 36 sc.

Rnd 6: Rep Rnd 5 = 48 sc.

Rnd 7: Work even.

Rnd 8: * Inc, sc in each of next 3 sc; rep from * around = 60 sc.

Rnd 9: Work even.

Rnd 10: Rep Rnd 8 = 75 sc.

Rnds 11 and 12: Work 2 rnds even.

Rnd 13: * Inc, sc in each of next 4 sc; rep from * around = 90 sc.

Rnds 14 through 17: Work 4 rnds even.

Rnd 18: Rep Rnd 13 = 108 sc.

Rnds 19 through 32: Work 14 rnds even. At end of Rnd 32, insert circular cardboard piece inside work and place at bottom.

Rnd 33: * Dec (decrease) over next 2 sc (**To work dec: Draw up a lp in each of next 2 sc, YO and draw through all 3 lps on hook = dec made**), sc in each of next 4 sc; rep from * around = 90 sc.

Rnds 34 and 35: Work 2 rnds even.

Rnd 36: * Dec, sc in each of next 3 sc; rep from * around = 72 sc.

Rnd 37: Work even.

Rnd 38: * Dec, sc in each of next 4 sc; rep from * around = 60 sc.

Rnd 39: Work even. Bottom section of body is now completed; continue with upper section as follows.

Rnd 40: * Inc, sc in each of next 4 sc; rep from * around = 72 sc.

Rnd 41: Work even.

Rnd 42: * Inc, sc in each of next 5 sc; rep from * around = 84 sc.

Rnd 43: Rep Rnd 42 = 98 sc.

Rnds 44 through 47: Work 4 rnds even.

Rnd 48: * Dec, sc in each of next 5 sc; rep from * around = 84 sc.

Rnds 49 through 51: Work 3 rnds even.

Rnd 52: * Dec, sc in each of next 5 sc; rep from * around = 72 sc.

Rnds 53 through 56: Work 4 rnds even.

Rnd 57: * Dec, sc in each of next 4 sc; rep from * around = 60 sc.

Rnd 58: Work even.

Rnd 59: * Dec, sc in each of next 4 sc; rep from * around = 50 sc.

Rnd 60: Work even.

Rnd 61: * Dec, sc in each of next 3 sc; rep from * around = 40 sc.

Rnd 62: * Dec, sc in each of next 2 sc; rep from * around = 30 sc.

Rnd 63: Work even. Upper section of body is now completed; continue with head as follows.

Rnd 64: * Inc, sc in each of next 2 sc; rep from * around = 40 sc.

Rnd 65: Work even.

Rnd 66: * Inc, sc in each of next 3 sc; rep from * around = 50 sc.

Rnd 67: * Inc, sc in each of next 4 sc; rep from * around = 60 sc.

Rnd 68: *Inc, sc in each of next 5 sc; rep from * around = 70 sc.

Rnds 69 through 73: Work 5 rnds even.

Rnd 74: * Dec, sc in each of next 5 sc, rep from * around = 60 sc.

Rnd 75: Work even.

Rnd 76: * Dec, sc in each of next 3 sc; rep from * around = 48 sc.

Rnds 77 and 78: Work 2 rnds even.

Rnd 79: * Dec, sc in each of next 2 sc; rep from * around = 36 sc.

Rnd 80: Work even. Now firmly stuff and shape body and head.

Rnd 81: * Dec, sc in next sc; rep from * around = 24 sc.

Rnd 82: Work even.

Rnd 83: Rep Rnd 81 = 16 sc.

Rnd 84: Work even. Finish stuffing head.

Rnd 85: * Dec; rep from * 7 times more = 8 sc. Finish off, leaving approx 6" end. Thread into tapestry or yarn needle; weave through sts of last rnd. Draw up tightly and fasten securely.

HAT: Beg at top, with larger size hook and Black, ch 2.

Rnd 1 (right side): Work 9 sc in 2nd ch from hook. Work continuous rnds (without joining); mark first st of rnd and move marker at beg of each rnd. Continue by working rnds on outside; right side of sts will be facing outside of hat.

Rnd 2: Work 2 sc in each sc around = 18 sc.

Rnd 3: * Sc in next sc, 2 sc in next sc (inc made); rep from * around = 27 sc.

Rnd 4: * Sc in each of next 2 sc, inc; rep from * around = 36 sc.

Rnd 5: * Sc in each of next 3 sc, inc; rep from * around = 45 sc.

Rnd 6: * Sc in each of next 4 sc, inc; rep from * around = 54 sc.

Rnd 7: Work even.

Rnd 8: Sc **in back lp** (lp away from you) of each sc around (ridge made). **Continue by working in both lps of sts.**

Rnds 9 through 18: Work 10 rnds even. Now continue with brim as follows.

Rnd 19: * Sc in each of next 5 sc, inc; rep from * around = 63 sc.

Rnd 20: Work even.

Rnd 21: * Sc in each of next 6 sc, inc; rep from * around = 72 sc.

Rnd 22: Work even. At end of rnd, join with a sl st in beg sc. Finish off; weave in ends. Place hat on top of head.

NOSE: With larger size hook and Hot Orange (*leave approx 12" length for sewing nose to snowman later*), ch 9.

Row 1: Sc in 2nd ch from hook and in each rem ch across = 8 sc.

Row 2: Ch 1, turn; sc in each sc to last sc, 2 sc in last sc = 9 sc.

Row 3: Ch 1, turn; sc in each sc across.

Row 4: Rep Row 2 = 10 sc.

Row 5: Rep Row 3.

Row 6: Ch 1, turn; sc in each sc to last sc, sl st in last sc.

Row 7: Ch 1, turn; sk sl st, sc in each rem sc across = 9 sc.

Rows 8 and 9: Rep Rows 6 and 7. At end of Row 9, finish off, leaving approx 12" sewing length. Thread into tapestry or yarn needle. Fold piece in half lengthwise; sew long edges and shaped edges at tip of nose tog. Stuff nose lightly. Thread beg length into tapestry or yarn needle and sew nose to center of face.

EYES (*make 2*): With larger size hook and Black, ch 3, join with a sl st to form a ring.

Rnd 1: Work 2 sc in each ch around, join with a sl st in beg sc = 6 sc. Finish off, leaving approx 4" sewing length. Sew eyes to face, having wrong side of sts facing up.

BUTTONS: With Black, make three 1½" diameter pompons (see instructions on page 11.) Attach pompons evenly spaced down center front of body.

SCARF: With larger size hook and Flame, ch 7.

Row 1 (wrong side): Sc in 2nd ch from hook and in each of next 4 chs; sc in last ch, changing to Golf Green. **[To change colors: Work sc until 2 lps rem on hook; drop old color (do not cut). With new color, YO and draw through both lps on hook = color changed.]**

Row 2: With Golf Green, ch 1, turn; carrying Flame across row and working over Golf Green yarn end (place strands on top of row and work following sts over them), sc in each sc across, changing to Flame in last sc (drop Golf Green, continue with Flame).

Row 3: With Flame, ch 1, turn; carrying Golf Green across row, sc in each sc across, changing to Golf Green in last sc.

Row 4: With Golf Green, ch 1, turn; carrying Flame across row, sc in each sc across, changing to Flame in last sc. Cut Golf Green.

Row 5: With Flame, ch 1, turn; working over Golf Green yarn end, sc in each sc across.

Row 6: Ch 1, turn; sc in each sc across. Rep Row 6 until scarf measures approx 34″ long, ending by working a wrong-side row, changing to Golf Green in last sc. Working in same manner as other stripes, work one row in each of the following colors: Golf Green, Flame, Golf Green and Flame (4 rows total). Finish off; weave in ends.

Fringe: With Flame, cut 12 strands, each 3″ long. With right side facing, knot one strand in each st across each short end of scarf (**Fig 1**). Tie scarf around neck.

HOLLY: Leaf: With Golf Green and smaller hook, ch 11. **Working in top lp of each ch**, sl st in 2nd ch from hook, sc in next ch; hdc in next ch, dc in next ch. Work picot as follows: Ch 3, sl st in 3rd ch from hook (*picot made*). Sc in next ch, hdc in next ch; dc in next ch, picot, sc in next ch; sl st in next ch, 3 sl sts in last ch. **Continuing to work on op-**

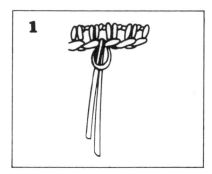

posite side of starting chain, sl st in next st, sc in next st; dc in next st, picot, sc in next st, hdc in next st; dc in next st, picot, sc in next st, sl st in each of last 3 sts. Finish off; weave in ends, leaving approx 6″ end for sewing.

Berries (*make 2*): With Flame and smaller hook, ch 2.

Rnd 1: Work 6 sc in 2nd ch from hook, do not join; work continuous rnds.

Rnd 2: Sc in each sc around.

Rnd 3: Rep Rnd 2. Finish off, leaving approx 6″ sewing length. Thread into tapestry or yarn needle and weave through last sts of rnd. Draw up tightly and fasten securely. Attach berries to leaf and sew to one side of hat, just above brim.

MR. AND MRS. S. CLAUS

designed by Kathie Schroeder

Make America's most popular couple as two stuffed dolls. This joyous pair, dressed in holiday finery, can be used as eye-catching Christmas decorations or to give a child lots of enjoyment during the holiday season.

Size

Approx 12½″ tall

Materials

Worsted weight yarn:
    8 oz red
    4 oz each white, pink, green and black
Synthetic mohair type yarn:
    4 oz white
Aluminum crochet hook size F (or size required for gauge)
Small amounts of felt in pink, black and red
22″ diameter circle of burlap
Polyester filling for stuffing
Two 1″ metal buckles
Five ⅝″ metal buttons
White craft glue
Tracing paper and pencil

Gauge

In hdc, 9 sts = 2″; 3 rnds/rows = 1″

S. CLAUS

Instructions

NOTE: Throughout patt, unless otherwise specified, do not join rnds; use a small safety pin or piece of yarn in contrasting color and mark first st of rnd; move marker at beg of each rnd. This will not be mentioned again in instructions.

LEFT BOOT AND LEG: With black, ch 2.

Rnd 1: Work 7 sc in 2nd ch from hook.

Rnd 2: Work 2 sc in each st around = 14 sc.

Rnd 3: Hdc in first st; (2 hdc in next st [inc made], hdc in next st) 6 times; inc in last st = 21 sts.

Rnd 4: Hdc in each of first 2 sts; (inc in next st, hdc in each of next 2 sts) 6 times; inc in last st = 28 sts.

Rnd 5: Hdc in **back lp only** (lp away from you—abbreviated BLO) of each st around.

Rnd 6: Working in both lps, hdc in each of first 9 sts, dec over next 2 sts. [**To work dec: YO, (insert hook in next st and draw up a lp) twice, YO**

and draw through all 4 lps now on hook = dec **made**]. Dec 4 times more, hdc in each of rem 9 sts = 23 sts.

Rnds 7 through 10: Hdc in each st around.

Rnd 11: Hdc in each st around to last st, change colors in last st. [**To change colors: Work a hdc until 3 lps are on hook; drop black, pick up red and complete the hdc with red = color changed.**] Finish off black and continue with red for leg.

Rnd 12: Hdc in each st around.

Rnd 13: Hdc in each st to last st; sc in last st, join with a sl st in first hdc of rnd. Do not remove marker from beg of rnd; it will be used later for joining. Finish off; weave in yarn ends. Set aside.

RIGHT BOOT AND LEG: Work as for Left Boot through Rnd 11.

Rnds 12 and 13: With red, hdc in each st around.

Rnd 14: Sc in each of first 9 sts.

Join legs at back as follows: Work a hdc in next st of **Right** Leg until 3 lps are on hook; pick up **Left** leg and insert hook in marked st of **Left** Leg; hook yarn and draw a lp through, YO and draw through all 4 lps now on hook. Remove marker from beg of rnd and place in st just made (for center back and beg of next rnd of Body); hdc in each of next 19 sts of **Left** Leg. [3 hdc are left unworked on Left Leg and you will now join legs at front.] On **Right** Leg, hdc in 4th st from joining st (marked st) at center back; continuing on **Right** Leg, hdc in each of next 18 sts. Do not finish off; you should now have 39 hdc and are ready to beg next rnd at center of back. Sew unworked sts between legs tog for crotch.

BODY: Rnd 15: Hdc in each of first 3 sts; (inc in next st, hdc in each of next 3 sts) 9 times = 48 sts.

Rnd 16: Hdc in first st, inc in next st; (hdc in each of next 4 sts, inc in next st) 9 times, hdc in last st = 58 sts.

Rnds 17 through 25: Hdc in each st around.

Rnd 26: Hdc in each of first 2 sts, dec as before; (hdc in each of next 4 sts, dec) 9 times = 48 sts.

Rnd 27: Dec over first 2 sts; (hdc in each of next 3 sts, dec) 9 times, hdc in last st = 38 sts.

Rnd 28: Hdc in each of first 2 sts; (dec, hdc in each of next 2 sts) 9 times = 29 sts.

Rnd 29: Hdc in first st; (dec, hdc in next st) 9 times, hdc in last st = 20 sts.

Finish off; weave in yarn ends.

BOOT TRIM (*make 2*): With white mohair type yarn, ch 30. Sc in 2nd ch from hook and in each ch across. Cut yarn, leaving approx 12″ sewing length. Sew to leg with right side of trim toward leg, wrong side facing you.

BELT: With black, ch 62.

Row 1: Hdc in 3rd ch from hook and in each ch across.

Row 2: Ch 2 (counts as one hdc), turn; hdc in each st across. Cut yarn, leaving approx 16″ sewing length. Run belt through buckle and sew to body at waist.

At this point, stuff boots, legs and body firmly. Shape stuffing so that Santa's tummy is pouched out. Set aside.

ARMS (make 2): With red, ch 2.

Rnd 1: Work 7 sc in 2nd ch from hook.

Rnd 2: Work 2 sc in each st around = 14 sc.

Rnd 3: Hdc in each st around.

Rnd 4: Hdc in each of first 2 sts, 4 hdc in next st, hdc in each of rem 11 sts = 17 sts.

Rnd 5: Hdc in each of first 2 sts, 2 hdc in each of next 4 sts, hdc in each of rem 11 sts = 21 sts.

Rnd 6: Hdc in each of first 2 sts; (dec over next 2 sts) 4 times, hdc in each of rem 11 sts = 17 sts.

Rnd 7: Hdc in each of first 2 sts, dec; hdc in each of rem 13 sts = 16 sts.

Rnds 8 through 13: Hdc in each st around.

Rnd 14: Hdc in each st to last st, sc in last st, sl st in beg hdc of rnd. Cut yarn, leaving approx 12″ sewing length.

SLEEVE CUFF (make 2): With white mohair type yarn, ch 20. Sc in 2nd ch from hook and in each ch across. Cut yarn, leaving approx 12″ sewing length. Sew to arm with right side of trim toward arm, wrong side facing you.

Stuff arms to within 1″ of opening; sew opening closed, then sew to body at Rnd 27 (3rd rnd from end).

HAT AND HEAD: With red, ch 2.

Rnd 1: Work 5 sc in 2nd ch from hook.

Rnd 2: Sc in each st around.

Rnd 3: Hdc in first sc; (inc in next sc, hdc in next sc) twice = 7 sts.

Rnds 4 and 5: Hdc in each st around.

Rnd 6: Hdc in first st; (inc in next st, hdc in next st) 3 times = 10 sts.

Rnds 7, 9, 11, 13, 15, 17 and 19. Hdc in each st around.

Rnd 8: Inc in first st, hdc in each of next 2 sts; inc in next st, hdc in next st; inc in next st, hdc in each of next 2 sts; inc in next st, hdc in last st = 14 sts.

Rnd 10: Hdc in first st; (inc in next st, hdc in next st) 6 times, inc in last st = 21 sts.

Rnd 12: Inc in first st; (hdc in each of next 2 sts, inc in next st) 6 times, hdc in each of last 2 sts = 28 sts.

Rnd 14: Hdc in each of first 3 sts; (inc in next st, hdc in each of next 3 sts) 6 times, inc in last st = 35 sts.

Rnd 16: Inc in first st; (hdc in each of next 4 sts, inc in next st) 6 times, hdc in each of last 4 sts = 42 sts.

Rnd 18: Hdc in each of first 5 sts; (inc in next st, hdc in each of next 5 sts) 6 times, inc in last st = 49 sts.

Rnd 20: Inc in first st; (hdc in each of next 6 sts, inc in next st) 6 times, hdc in each of last 6 sts = 56 sts.

Rnd 21: Hdc in each st around, changing to pink in last st (as in Rnd 11 of Boot). Finish off red; continue with pink.

Head: Rnd 22: Hdc in each st around.

Rnd 23: Hdc in each of first 5 sts; (dec, hdc in each of next 5 sts) 7 times, dec over last 2 sts = 48 sts.

Rnd 24: Hdc in each of first 2 sts, dec; (hdc in each of next 4 sts, dec) 7 times, hdc in each of last 2 sts = 40 sts.

Rnd 25: Dec over first 2 sts; (hdc in each of next 3 sts, dec) 7 times, hdc in each of last 3 sts = 32 sts.

Rnd 26: Hdc in each of first 2 sts; (dec, hdc in each of next 2 sts) 7 times, dec over last 2 sts = 24 sts. Before working next rnd, stuff hat lightly to within 3″ of tip; fold 3″ unstuffed tip to side of hat, leaving tip free to attach pompon later. Stuff head firmly.

Rnd 27: Dec over first 2 sts; (hdc in next st, dec) 7 times, sc in last st, sl st in beg hdc of rnd. Finish off; weave in yarn ends.

HAT TRIM: With white mohair type yarn, ch 46.

Row 1: Hdc in 3rd ch from hook and in each ch across.

Row 2: Ch 2, turn; hdc in each st across. Cut yarn, leaving approx 20″ sewing length. Sew to hat in same manner as boot and sleeve trim.

NECK (hidden by beard in photo): With white mohair type yarn, ch 31.

Row 1: Hdc in 3rd ch from hook and in each ch across.

Rows 2 and 3: Ch 2 (counts as one hdc), turn; hdc in each st across. Cut yarn, leaving 16″ sewing length.

Sew beg edge of neck to body and sew seam at

center back; stuff lightly. Sew top edge of neck to head.

HAIR: With white mohair type yarn, ch 17.

Row 1: Beg in 2nd ch from hook and work one lp st in each ch across (see **Fig 1** for lp st instructions) = 16 lp sts.

Row 2: Ch 1, turn; sc in each st across = 16 sc.

Row 3: Ch 1, turn; work a lp st in each sc across.

Rows 4 through 8: Rep Rows 2 and 3 twice, then rep Row 2 once more. Cut yarn, leaving approx 12″ sewing length. Sew to back of head below hat and tack on each side to face.

BEARD: With white mohair type yarn, ch 5.

Row 1: Beg in 2nd ch from hook and work a lp st in each ch across = 4 lp sts.

Row 2: Ch 1, turn; inc in first st, sc in each st to last st, inc in last st = 6 sc.

Row 3: Ch 1, turn; work a lp st in each sc across.

Rows 4 through 17: Rep Rows 2 and 3 seven times. At end of Row 17, you should have 20 sts. Cut yarn, leaving approx 12″ sewing length. Sew to head above neck.

MRS. CLAUS

Instructions

NOTE: Throughout patt, unless otherwise specified, do not join rnds; mark beg of rnd and move marker at beg of each rnd. This will not be mentioned again in instructions.

LEFT BOOT AND LEG: With black, ch 2.

Rnds 1 through 6: Rep Rnds 1 through 6 of Santa's Boot, changing to white in last st (as in Rnd 11 of Santa's Boot). You should have 23 sts. Finish off black; continue with white for leg.

Rnds 7 and 8: Hdc in each st around.

Rnd 9: Hdc in back lp only (lp away from you—abbreviated BLO) of each st around.

Rnd 10 through 12: Hdc in both lps of each st around.

Rnd 13: Rep Rnd 13 of Santa's Left Boot and Leg. Finish off; weave in yarn ends. Set aside.

RIGHT BOOT AND LEG: Work as for Left Boot and leg through Rnd 12.

Rnd 13: Hdc in each st around.

Rnd 14. Rep Rnd 14 of Santa's Right Boot and Leg; do not finish off.

BODY: Rnds 15 and 16: Continuing with white, rep Rnds 15 and 16 of Santa's Body.

---

1   **LOOP STITCH**

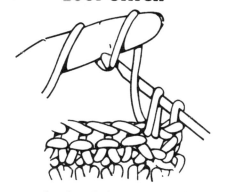

With wrong side of work facing, insert hook into st; hook yarn and draw a lp through st. Wrap yarn around tip of left-hand index finger, insert hook behind yarn and through lp on finger; draw lp through one lp on hook.

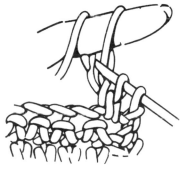

Insert hook in front of lp on finger and in back of yarn; hook yarn and draw yarn through rem lps on hook. Drop long lp off finger.

Rnds 17 through 19: Hdc in each st around.

Rnd 20: Hdc in each st around, changing to red in last st.

Rnd 21: Hdc in each st around.

Rnd 22: Hdc in BLO of each st around.

Rnds 23 through 25: Hdc in both lps of each st around.

Rnds 26 through 29; Rep Rnds 26 through 29 of Santa's Body. Finish off; weave in yarn ends.

LACE TRIM FOR BLOOMERS (*make 2*): With center back of leg facing you, join white mohair type yarn with a sl st in an unworked lp of Rnd 8 of Leg. Ch 2, 2 dc in same st as joining, * sl st in next st, 3 dc in next st; rep from * around, join with a sl st in top of beg ch-2. Finish off; weave in yarn ends.

PEPLUM (*extension of garment below the waist*): Hold Body upside down with front facing you. Join red with a sl st in unworked lp of Rnd 21 of Body at center of front.

Row 1: Ch 1, hdc in same st as joining, hdc in each of next 57 sts = 58 sts.

Row 2: Ch 1 turn; sc in first st, hdc in each st to last st, sc in last st.

Rows 3 through 11: Rep Row 2 nine times,

Row 12: Ch 1, turn; sc in first st, sk next st, hdc in each st to last 2 sts; sk next st, sc in last st = 56 sts.

Row 13: Rep Row 12 = 54 sts. Finish off; weave in yarn ends.

TRIM: With wrong side of Peplum facing you, beg at waist (top of right front opening edge), and join white mohair type yarn with a sl st in end st of first row of Peplum.

Row 1: Sc in same st as joining, sc in end st of each of next 11 rows, work 3 sc (for corner) in end st of last row; now working along bottom, sc in each of next 54 sts; work 3 sc for corner, sc in end st of each rem row up left front opening.

Row 2: Do not ch, turn; sc in each sc around entire edge, join with a sl st in last st at waist. Finish off; weave in yarn ends.

BELT: Rep instructions for Santa's belt. Attach buckle and sew to body at waist. Stuff boots, legs and body.

ARMS AND SLEEVE CUFFS (*make 2 each*): Rep instructions for Santa's Arms and Sleeve Cuffs. Stuff arms to within 1″ of opening, sew opening closed. Sew arms to body at Rnd 27 (3rd rnd from end).

HEAD: With pink ch 2.

Rnd 1: Work 7 sc in 2nd ch from hok.

Rnd 2: Work 2 sc in each st around = 14 sc.

Rnd 3: Hdc in first st; (2 hdc in next st [inc made], hdc in next st) 6 times, inc in last st = 21 hdc.

Rnd 4: Hdc in each of first 2 sts; (inc in next st, hdc in each of next 2 sts) 6 times, inc in last st = 28 sts.

Rnd 5: Inc in first st; (hdc in each of next 3 sts, inc in next st) 6 times, hdc in each of last 3 sts = 35 sts.

Rnd 6: Hdc in each of first 4 sts; (inc in next st, hdc in each of next 4 sts) 6 times, inc in last st = 42 sts.

Rnd 7: Hdc in each of first 2 sts; (inc in next st, hdc in each of next 9 sts) 4 times = 46 sts.

Rnds 8 through 11: Hdc in each st around.

Rnd 12: Hdc in each of first 2 sts: (dec, hdc in each of next 9 sts) 4 times = 42 sts.

Rnd 13: Hdc in each of first 4 sts; (dec, hdc in each of next 4 sts) 6 times, dec over last 2 sts = 35 sts.

Rnd 14: Dec over first 2 sts; (hdc in each of next 3 sts, dec) 6 times, hdc in each of last 3 sts = 28 sts.

Rnd 15: Hdc in first st; (dec, hdc in each of next 2 sts) 6 times, dec; hdc in last st, changing to white mohair type yarn = 21 sts. Finish off pink; continue with white mohair type yarn.

NECK: Rnd 16: Hdc in BLO of each st around.

Rnds 17 and 18: Hdc in both lps of each st around. Cut yarn, leaving approx 16″ sewing length.

Stuff and sew to stuffed body.

LACE NECK EDGING: With center back of neck facing you, join white mohair type yarn with a sl st in unworked lp of Rnd 15 of Head. Ch 2, 2 dc in same st as joining; (sl st in next st, 3 dc in next st) 10 times, join with a sl st in top of beg ch-2. Finish off; weave in yarn ends.

COIFFURE: Cut 90 strands of white mohair type yarn, each 14″ long. Separate into fifteen 6-strand groups. Using the backstitch sewing method, sew the groups at midpoint of strands at center on top of head (**Fig 2**). Beg at forehead and attach each group (with only one backstitch for each group, please!) behind the prev group. This forms a "part" in the hair.

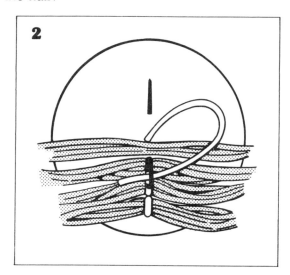

Bring yarn ends of groups around to back of head; gather and tie them into a "pony tail" using an 8″ length of yarn; do not finish off. Tuck groups of yarn ends under to form a "bun" and use ends of the 8″ length to secure in place (**Fig 3**). Finish off; weave in yarn ends.

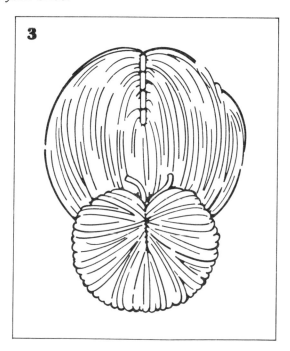

EAR MUFFS (make 2): With red, ch 2.

Rnd 1: Work 7 sc in 2nd ch from hook.

Rnd 2: Work 2 sc in each st around = 14 sc.

Rnd 3: Sc in first st; (inc in next st, sc in next st) 6 times, inc in last st = 21 sc.

Rnd 4: Sc in first st, sc in BLO of each rem st around, join with a sl st in BLO of first sc of rnd. Finish off; weave in yarn ends.

Band: With black, ch 33; sc in 2nd ch from hook and in each ch across. Ch 1, turn; sc in each st across. Finish off; weave in yarn ends. Sew ear muffs and band to head.

HOLLY APPLIQUE: Berries (make 8): With red, ch 2.

Rnd 1: Work 6 sc in 2nd ch from hook.

Rnd 2: Sc in each sc around.

Rnd 3: (Dec over 2 sts) 3 times. Cut yarn, leaving approx 6″ sewing length.

Leaves (make 8): With green, ch 11.

Row 1: Working in one lp only of each ch, sl st in 2nd ch from hook, sc in next ch, hdc in next ch; † dc in next ch, ch 3, sl st in first ch of ch-3 just made †; sc in next ch, hdc in next ch, rep from † to † once; sc in next ch, sl st in next ch, 3 sl sts in last ch.

Next Row: Turning piece slightly and working on opposite side of starting ch, sl st in first ch; sc in next ch, rep from † to † of Row 1; sc in next ch, hdc in next ch; rep from † to † once, sc in next ch; sl st in each of last 3 chs. Cut yarn, leaving approx 6″ sewing length.

Finishing

Place tracing paper over **Fig 4**; with pencil, trace over outlines for eyes, cheeks and nose—mouth for Mrs. Claus only. Cut outlines just traced and use as patterns on felt. Refer to photo for positions of facial features; glue felt pieces to face.

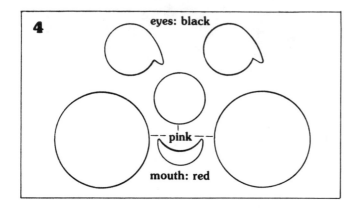

4

eyes: black

pink

mouth: red

Sew on buttons; Santa has 3 buttons, one below belt and 2 evenly spaced above belt. Mrs. Claus has only 2 buttons. Make a 1½″ pompon *(see page 11)* and attach to tip of Santa's hat.

Sew a holly applique of 2 leaves and 2 berries to Santa's hat. For Santa's bag, use the circle of burlap tied at top with 12″ length of red yarn; attach second applique with same red yarn used for tying.

Sew one holly applique to lower left corner of Peplum and one in hair behind left ear muff on Mrs. Claus.

(Opposite) Mr. and Mrs. S. Claus - page 59

Snowman - page 54

Puppy Dog Stocking - page 95

(Opposite) Reindeer Christmas Card Holder - page 25

Giant Ribbed Christmas Stockings - page 98

Snowflakes - page 21

Clancey Clown - page 133

(Opposite) Christmas Puppy - page 43 / Snowlady and Snowman - page 47 / Santa Mouse - page 51

Set the Christmas Table - page 31

(Opposite) Poinsettia Afghan - page 105

Tree Top Angel - page 13

Dog Christmas Coat - page 115

Holly Ornament - page 121

(Opposite) Covered Tree Ornaments - page 17
Popcorn and Cranberry Garland - page 23
Tiny Treasures - page 119

Braided Christmas Wreath - page 37

Baby's Santa Hat - page 116

Christmas Wreath - page 29

Baby's Santa Bib - page 117

(Opposite) Portrait Pillows - page 33 / Santa Sock - page 101 / Santa Gift Tote - page 111

Sister Sue and Her Basket, Too - page 129

Brother and Sister Dolls - page 137

(Opposite) Snow Clusters Baby Afghan - page 107

Big Bear - page 123

Mouse Toy - page 142

(Opposite) Christmas Angel Wall Hanging - page 39

WORSTED WEIGHT

SPORT WEIGHT

CHRISTMAS CAROLERS

designed by Sue Penrod

This charming scene of carolers can be used as a holiday centerpiece, on a mantel, or just about anywhere. Make them either in sport weight yarn or worsted weight yarn. Our directions include instructions for both types of yarn. Be sure to achieve gauge as specified for the particular yarn. If you do not have the correct number of stitches per inch, your work will not fit over the styrofoam forms and will not look exactly as shown.

Size

Approx height:	Sport Weight	Worsted Weight
girl	6″	8″
boy	6″	8″
lady	8″	10″
man	9″	12″
dog	3″	4″
lamp post	10½″	13½″

Materials

Yarn:

black	2 oz	3 oz
red	1 oz	2 oz
lime green	½ oz	1 oz
medium green	1 oz	2 oz
light brown	½ oz	1 oz
dark brown	1 oz	2 oz
light yellow	½ oz	1 oz
bright yellow	½ oz	1 oz
light pink	1 oz	2 oz
white	½ oz	1 oz

Aluminum crochet hook size (or size required for gauge):	D	F
Styrofoam forms (see Note below):		
4″ cones	2	—
6″	2	2
8″	—	2
1″ diameter rod	8″ length	10″ length
Metal ring	2″ diameter	2½″ diameter

Polyester fiber (for stuffing)

Small felt pieces in black, red and white

Tracing paper and pencil

White craft glue

4 Pieces of white paper, each 1½″ x 2″, folded in half the long way (for songsheets)

6 Red beads (5mm diameter)

Straight round-head pins: 4 light green, 6 white and 1 pearl (11 total)

Size 16 tapestry needle

(Opposite) Christmas Carolers

NOTE: Styrofoam cuts easily with a sharp knife. If unable to find sizes specified, buy larger size and cut off excess at base of cone or at end of rod.

Gauge

With sport weight yarn and size D hook, 5 sc = 1″
With worsted weight yarn and size F hook, 9 sc = 2″

General Instructions

Unless otherwise specified, work continuous rnds throughout each pattern. Do not join rnds; do not chain and turn. Use a small safety pin or piece of yarn in contrasting color and mark first st of rnd; move marker at beg of each rnd.

Follow instructions carefully. Each pattern will specify working in back lp (lp away from you—abbreviated BL), in front lp (lp toward you—abbreviated FL) or in both lps of sts (*see Fig 1*).

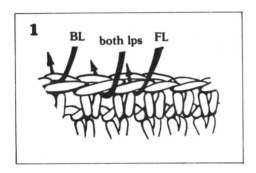

Use size D hook with sport weight yarn or size required to obtain 5 sts per inch. Use size F hook with worsted weight yarn or size required to obtain 9 sts per 2 inches. Do not hesitate to change to larger or smaller hook if necessary to achieve gauge. If you have more sts per inch than specified, try a larger size hook. If you have less sts per inch then specified, try a smaller size hook.

GIRL CAROLER

Before proceeding, read General Instructions.

HEAD: With pink, ch 4, join with a sl st to form a ring.

Rnd 1: Work 2 sc in each ch around = 8 sc.

Rnd 2: Work 2 sc in BL (back lp) of each sc around = 16 sc.

Rnd 3: Rep Rnd 2 = 32 sc.

Rnds 4, 5 and 6: Sc in Bl of each sc around.

Rnd 7: Working in BL of each sc, * sc in each of next 2 sc, sk one sc, sc in next sc; rep from * around = 24 sc.

Rnd 8: * Sc in BL of next sc, sk one sc, sc in BL of next sc; rep from * around = 16 sc. Before working next rnd, lightly stuff and shape head. [*NOTE: Stuffing should not be visible through sts.*]

Rnd 9: * Sk one sc, sc in BL of next sc; rep from * to last sc; sc in BL of last sc, changing to white. [**To Change Colors: Work sc until 2 lps rem on hook; cut color being used, tie in new color and complete st (YO and draw through 2 lps on hook) = color changed.**] You should now have 8 sc; continue with white and work collar as follows.

COLLAR: Rnd 1: Working in BL of each sc, * sc in next sc, 2 sc in next sc; rep from * around = 12 sc.

Rnd 2: Rep Rnd 1 = 18 sc.

Rnd 3 (edging): * Sc in FL (front lp) of next sc, ch 2; rep from * to last sc; sc in FL of last sc, changing to red (as before). Continue with red and work coat as follows.

COAT: Rnd 1: Hold collar edging back toward you and work in unused (back) lp of each sc (behind collar edging) as follows. *Sc in next sc, 2 sc in next sc; rep from * around = 27 sc.

Rnd 2: Sc in BL of each sc around.

Rnd 3 (marking rnd): Working in BL of each sc, sc in each of next 6 sc; * **in next sc, work sc in BL and mark FL (use marker different from beg of rnd) for sewing sleeve to coat later** * ; sc in each of next 13 sc; rep from * to * once; sc in each of rem 6 sc.

Rnds 4 through 9: Sc in BL of each sc around.

Rnd 10: Working in BL of each sc, * sc in each of next 2 sc, 2 sc in next sc; rep from * around = 36 sc.

Rnds 11 and 12: Sc in BL of each sc around.

Rnd 13: Rep Rnd 10 = 48 sc.

Rep Rnd 2, three times more for sport weight yarn, or five times more for worsted weight yarn.

Next Rnd (edging): * Ch 1, sc in FL of next sc; rep from * around. Continue edging up front center of coat as follows. Hold work with head to your left and last st worked to your right. * Ch 1, insert hook from right to left under front (unused) lp of st in next rnd (directly to the left of last st worked) and work one sc; rep from * to last rnd of white at neck. [NOTE: Edging is worked across collar edging at end of rnd.] Finish off; weave in end.

SKIRT TRIM AND BASE: Hold bottom edge of coat across top with bottom edging back toward you. Join white with a sl st in unused (back) lp of back center sc (behind edging).

Rnd 1: Working in unused lp of each sc (behind edging), ch 1, sc in same st as joining and in each rem sc around = 48 sc.

Rnd 2 (skirt trim): * Sc in FL of next sc, ch 2; rep from * around.

Rnd 3: Hold skirt trim back toward you and work sc in unused (back) lp of each sc (behind skirt trim) around = 48 sc.

Rnd 4: Working in BL of each sc around, * sc in each of next 2 sc, sk one sc, sc in next sc; rep from * around = 36 sc. Before working next rnd, insert 4" cone for sport weight yarn, or 6" cone for worsted weight yarn inside of coat.

Rnd 5: * Sc in BL of next sc, sk one sc, sc in BL of next sc; rep from * around = 24 sc.

Rnd 6 * Sk one sc, sc in BL of next sc; rep from * around = 12 sc.

Rnd 7: Rep Rnd 6 = 6 sc. Finish off, leaving approx 6" end. Thread into tapestry needle; weave

through sts of last rnd. Draw up tightly and fasten securely.

SLEEVE AND HAND (make 2): With red, leave approx 12" end for sewing to coat later, ch 10; join with a sl st to form a ring.

Rnd 1: Sc in each ch around = 10 sc.

Rnds 2 through 8: Sc in both lps of each sc around = 10 sc. At end of Rnd 8, change to white in last sc.

Rnd 9 (sleeve trim): With white, * sc in FL of next sc, ch 2; rep from * to last sc; sc in FL of last sc, changing to pink for hand.

Rnd 10: Hold sleeve trim back toward you. With pink, work sc in unused (back) lp of each sc (behind trim) around = 10 sc.

Rnd 11: * Sc in both lps of next sc, sk one sc; rep from * around = 5 sc. Finish off, leaving approx 6" end. Thread into tapestrty needle; weave through sts of last rnd. Draw up tightly and fasten securely.

[NOTE: At end of second sleeve and hand, tack end of both hands tog before finishing off.] Sew beg open edge of sleeve tog, carefully matching 5 corresponding sc across. Then sew this edge to side of coat below marker.

BONNET AND HAIR: With red, ch 4, join with a sl st to form a ring.

Rnd 1: Work 2 sc in each ch around = 8 sc.

Rnd 2: Work 2 sc in both lps of each sc around = 16 sc.

Rnd 3: Working in both lps of each sc, (sl st, ch 3, dc) in next sc, dc in next sc; * 2 dc in next sc, dc in next sc; rep from * around, join with a sl st in top of beg ch-3 = 24 dc (counting ch-3).

Rnd 4: Ch 3, dc in BL of next dc and in each rem dc around; join with a sl st in top of beg ch-3.

Rnds 5, 6 and 7: Ch 3, dc in both lps of next dc and in each rem dc around; join with a sl st in top of beg ch-3.

Rnd 8 (brim): Ch 1, turn; working in BL of each st, sc in each of next 2 dc; * 2 dc in next dc, dc in next dc; rep from * to last 5 dc; dc in next dc, sc in each of rem 4 dc; join with a sl st in both lps of beg sc. Finish off; weave in end.

Rnd 9 (hair): Turn; with outside of bonnet facing you and brim edge across top, fold brim back toward you and work in unused lp of each st (behind brim) as follows. Sk first 4 sc from joining of prev rnd, join dk brown with a sl st in next dc; ch 1, sc in same st; * ch 4, sc in next dc; rep from * to last 2 sc (leave rem 2 sc—6 total—unworked). Finish off; weave in ends. Unfold brim and place bonnet with attached hair on head.

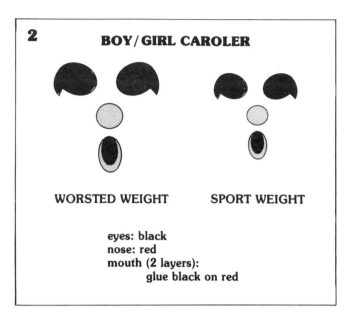

2

BOY/GIRL CAROLER

WORSTED WEIGHT   SPORT WEIGHT

eyes: black
nose: red
mouth (2 layers):
    glue black on red

Finishing

Facial Features: Trace outlines in **Fig 2** on paper. Cut outlines and use as patterns on felt as indicated. With glue, attach felt pieces as shown in photo.

Buttons: Insert 6 white-head straight pins into body evenly spaced down front center edging of coat.

Place songsheet in arms.

BOY CAROLER

Before proceeding, read General Instructions.

HEAD: Work same as Girl Caroler, changing to dk brown (instead of white) in last sc of Rnd 9. Continue with dk brown and work coat as follows.

COAT: Rnd 1: * Sc in BL of next sc, 2 sc in BL of next sc; rep from * around = 12 sc.

Rnd 2: Rep Rnd 1 = 18 sc.

Rnd 3: Rep Rnd 1 = 27 sc.

Rnds 4 through 15: Rep Rnds 2 through 13 of *Coat instructions for Girl Caroler.*

Rnd 16: Sc in BL of each sc around.

Rep Rnd 16, twice more for sport weight yarn, or four times more for worsted weight yarn.

Next Rnd (edging): Work hdc in FL of each sc around to last sc, work 2 hdc in FL of last sc. Continue edging up front center of coat and around neck as follows. Hold work with head to your left and last st worked to your right. * Insert hook from

right to left under front (unused) lp of st in next rnd (directly to the left of last st worked) and work one hdc; rep from * across center front, ending by working 2 hdc in last rnd of brown at neck. Continue edging around neck; with head away from you, work to your left in last rnd of brown as follows. Work hdc in unused lp of each sc around neck. Finish off; weave end into front center edging.

BASE: Hold bottom edge of coat across top with bottom edging back toward you. Join dk brown with a sl st in unused (back) lp of back center sc (behind bottom edging).

Rnd 1: Working in unused lp of each sc (behind edging), ch 1, sc in same st as joining and in each rem sc around = 48 sc. [*NOTE: Bottom edging remains folded up toward neck.*]

Rnd 2: Sc in BL of each sc around.

Rnds 3 through 6: Rep Rnds 4 through 7 of *Skirt Trim and Base Instructions for Girl Caroler.*

SLEEVE AND HAND (*make 2*): With dk brown, work same as Girl Caroler to Rnd 9. Do not change to white in last sc of Rnd 8; continue with dk brown.

Rnd 9 (edging): Hdc in FL of each sc to last sc; sc in FL of last sc, changing to pink for hand.

Rnds 10 and 11: Rep Rnds 10 and 11 of *Sleeve and Hand instructions for Girl Caroler*. Complete in same manner as Girl Caroler.

CAP AND HAIR: With dk brown, ch 4, join with a sl st to form a ring.

Rnd 1: Work 2 sc in each ch around = 8 sc.

Rnd 2: Work 2 sc in BL of each sc around = 16 sc.

Rnd 3: Working in BL of each sc, sc in next sc; * 2 sc in next sc, sc in each of next 2 sc; rep from * around = 21 sc.

Rnd 4: Working in BL of each sc, * 2 sc in next sc, sc in each of next 2 sc; rep from * around = 28 sc.

Rnds 5, 6 and 7: Sc in BL of each sc around.

Rnd 8: Sc in FL of each sc around (back lp will be used later for working hair).

Rnd 9: (visor): Working in both lps of each sc, sc in each of next 11 sc, 2 hdc in next sc; 2 dc in each of next 4 sc; 2 hdc in next sc; sc in each of rem 11 sc; join with a sl st in both lps of beg sc. Finish off; weave in ends.

Rnd 10 (hair): Fold last 3 rnds back toward you and work in unused lp of each sc of Rnd 7 (inside of cap) as follows. Join lt yellow with a sl st in back center sc, ch 1; work loop stitch (***Fig 3***) in same st as joining and in each rem sc around. [NOTE: *Each loop should measure approx ¾″ long.*] Join with a sl st in beg loop stitch. Finish off; weave in ends. Unfold last 3 rnds of cap and place cap with attached hair on top of head. Tack in place, if desired.

SCARF: With med green, ch 50. Dc in 4th ch from hook and in each rem ch across. Finish off; weave in ends. Tie scarf around neck, just below neck edging with ends of scarf at side (one at front and one at back).

Finishing

Make facial features same as for Girl Caroler. Place songsheet in arms.

LADY CAROLER

Before proceeding, read General Instructions.

HEAD: Work same as Girl Caroler to Rnd 7.

Rnds 7 and 8: Sc in BL of each sc around.

---

3 **LOOP STITCH**

Insert hook in st, hook yarn and draw lp through (2 lps now on hook). Wrap yarn twice around tip of left index finger, insert hook in front of yarn and through first lp on finger.

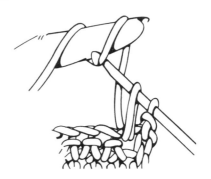

Hook yarn and draw lp through one lp on hook. Bring left index finger down in front of work, skip first lp on finger and insert hook through second lp on finger.

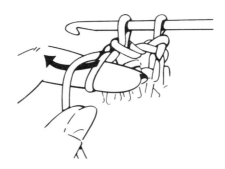

Hook yarn and draw lp through both rem lps on hook. Drop long lp off finger.

Rnd 9: Working in BL of each sc, * sc in each of next 2 sc, sk one sc, sc in next sc; rep from * around = 24 sc.

Rnd 10: Rep Rnd 9 = 18 sc.

Rnd 11: Working in BL of each sc, sc in next sc; * sk one sc, sc in each of next 3 sc; rep from * to last sc; sc in last sc, changing to med green for coat = 14 sc. Before working next rnd, lightly stuff and shape head.

COAT: Rnd 1: Sc in BL of each sc around = 14 sc.

Rnd 2: Working in BL of each sc, sc in each of next 2 sc; * 2 sc in next sc, sc in each of next 3 sc; rep from * around = 17 sc.

Rnd 3: Working in BL of each sc, sc in next sc; * 2 sc in next sc, sc in each of next 3 sc; rep from * around = 21 sc.

Rnd 15: Working in BL of each sc, sc in each of next 3 sc; * 2 sc in next sc, sc in each of next 3 sc; rep from * around = 38 sc.

Rnds 16, 17 and 18: Sc in BL of each sc around.

Rnd 19: Working in BL of each sc, sc in each of next 2 sc; * 2 sc in next sc, sc in each of next 3 sc; rep from * around = 47 sc.

Rnds 20 through 24: Sc in BL of each sc around. At end of Rnd 24, join with a sl st in both lps of beg sc.

Rnd 25 (edging): Ch 3, dc in FL of same sc as joining and each rem sc around to last sc, 2 dc in FL of last sc. Continue edging up front center of coat, around neck, and then down front center of coat as follows. Hold work with head to your left and last st worked to your right. * Insert hook from right to left under front (unused) lp of st in next rnd (directly to the left of last st worked) and work one dc; rep from * across center front, ending by working 2 dc in last rnd of med green at neck. Continue edging around neck; with head away from you, work to your left in last rnd of med green as follows. Work dc in unused lp of each sc around neck, ending by working 2 dc in last st before center edging. Now continue edging down center front (next to other edging); work dc in unused lp of each sc down front to bottom edging, join with a sl st in top of beg ch-3. Finish off; weave in end. [NOTE: *Bottom edging should be folded up toward head and neck edging should be folded down toward bottom edge.*]

DRESS TRIM AND BASE: Hold bottom edge of coat across top with bottom edging back toward you. Join lime green with a sl st in unused (back) lp of back center sc (behind edging).

Rnd 1: Working in unused lp of each sc (behind edging), ch 1, sc in same st as joining and in each rem sc around = 47 sc.

Rnd 2 (dress trim): * Ch 2, sc in FL of next sc; rep from * around.

Rnd 3: Hold dress trim back toward you and work sc in unused lp of each sc (behind trim) around = 47 sc.

Rnds 4 and 5: Rep Rnds 2 and 3.

Rnds 6 and 7: Sc in BL of each sc around = 47 sc.

Rnd 8: Working in BL of each sc, sc in each of next 3 sc; * sk one sc, sc in each of next 3 sc; rep from * around = 36 sc. Before working next rnd, insert 6" cone for sport weight yarn, or 8" cone for worsted weight yarn inside of coat.

Rnd 9: Working in BL of each sc, * sc in each of

Rnd 4 (marking rnd): Working in BL of each sc, sc in next sc, 2 sc in next sc, sc in each of next 2 sc; * **in next sc, work sc in BL and mark FL (use marker different from beg of rnd) for sewing sleeve to coat later** *; work (2 sc in next sc, sc in each of next 3 sc) twice, 2 sc in next sc; rep from * to * once; sc in each of next 2 sc, 2 sc in next sc, sc in each of rem 3 sc = 26 sc.

Rnd 5: Working in BL of each sc, sc in next sc; * 2 sc in next sc, sc in each of next 4 sc; rep from * around = 31 sc.

Rnds 6 through 14: Sc in BL of each sc around.

next 2 sc, sk one sc, sc in next sc; rep from *
around = 27 sc.

Rnd 10: Rep Rnd 8 = 21 sc.

Rnd 11: Working in BL of each sc, sc in next sc; * sk one sc, sc in each of next 3 sc; rep from * around = 16 sc.

Rnd 12: * Sk one sc, sc in BL of next sc; rep from * around = 8 sc. Finish off, leaving approx 6" end. Thread into tapestry needle; weave through sts of last rnd. Draw up tightly and fasten securely.

SLEEVE AND HAND (make 2): With med green, leave approx 12" end for sewing to coat later, ch 12; join with a sl st to form a ring.

Rnd 1: Sc in each ch around = 12 sc.

Rnds 2 through 8: Sc in both lps of each sc around.

Rnd 9 (marking rnd): In next sc, work sc in FL and mark BL (use marker different from beg of rnd) for working hand later; sc in FL of each sc around to last sc; sc in FL of last sc, changing to lime green (do not cut med green). [NOTE: Back lps are used later for working hand.]

Rnd 10 (sleeve trim): With lime green, * sc in BL of next sc, ch 2; rep from * to last sc; sc in BL of last sc, changing to med green (finish off lime green).

Rnd 11 (edging): With med green and working in unused (front) lp of each sc (in front of sleeve trim), hdc in each sc to last sc; sc in last sc, join with a sl st in both lps of beg hdc. Finish off; weave in ends.

Hand: Fold last 3 rnds back toward you and join pink with a sl st in marked lp.

Rnd 1: Working in unused lp of each sc in same rnd as marked lp, sc in same st as joining and in each rem st around = 12 sc.

Rnds 2, 3 and 4: Sc in both lps of each sc around.

Rnd 5: * Sk one sc, sc in both lps of next sc; rep from * around = 6 sc. Finish off, leaving approx 6" end. Thread into tapestry needle; weave through sts of last rnd. Draw up tightly and fasten securely; unfold last 3 rnds of sleeve. [NOTE: At end of second sleeve and hand, tack end of both hands tog before finishing off.] Sew beg open edge of sleeve tog, carefully matching 6 corresponding sc across. Then sew this edge to side of coat below marker.

BONNET AND HAIR: With med green, ch 4, join with a sl st to form a ring.

Rnd 1: Work 2 sc in each ch around = 8 sc.

Rnd 2: * Sc in BL of next sc, 2 sc in BL of next sc; rep from * around = 12 sc.

Rnd 3: Rep Rnd 2 = 18 sc.

Rnd 4: Rep Rnd 2 = 27 sc.

Rnds 5 through 10: Sc in BL of each sc around. At end of Rnd 10, join with a sl st in both lps of beg sc. Drop med green (do not cut); join lime green.

Rnd 11: With lime green, ch 1, sc in BL of same st as joining and in each rem sc around; join with a sl st in both lps of beg sc.

Rnd 12: Rep Rnd 11. At end of rnd, finish off lime green; continue with med green.

Rnd 13 (brim): In same sc as joining, * **work sc in FL and mark BL (use marker different from beg of rnd) for working hair later.** * Continue working in FL of each sc as follows (back lps will be used later for working hair). Sc in next sc, hdc in next sc, dc in next sc; work (2 dc in next sc, dc in next sc) 7 times; hdc in next sc, sc in next sc; in next sc, rep from * to * once (rem 6 sc are left unworked).

Rnd 14 (brim edging): Ch 1, turn; working in both lps of each st, sk first sc, sc in next st; * ch 1, sc in next st; rep from * to last sc, sl st in last sc. Finish off; weave in ends.

Hair: Do not turn; with inside of bonnet facing you and 6 unworked sc at back of neck across top, fold brim away from you and join light yellow with a sl st in marked lp to the left of unworked sts at back of neck. Working in unused lp of each sc in same rnd as marked lps, sc in same lp as joining; * ch 4, sc in next sc; rep from * around, ending in other marked lp. Finish off; weave in ends. Unfold brim and place bonnet with attached hair on head.

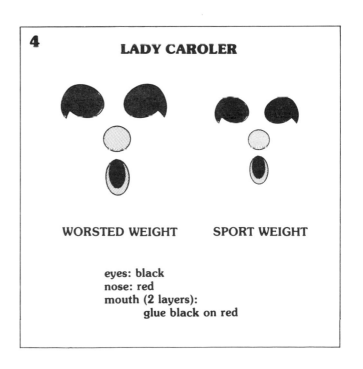

4

LADY CAROLER

WORSTED WEIGHT   SPORT WEIGHT

eyes: black
nose: red
mouth (2 layers):
    glue black on red

Finishing

Facial Features: Trace outlines in *Fig 4* on paper. Cut outlines and use as patterns on felt as indicated. With glue, attach felt pieces as shown in photo.

Buttons: Insert 8 green-head straight pins into body evenly spaced down front in center of edging.

Place songsheet in arms.

MAN CAROLER

Before proceeding, read General Instructions.

HEAD: Work same as Lady Caroler, changing to white (instead of med green) in last sc of Rnd 11. Before working next rnd, lightly stuff and shape head. Continuing with white, work collar as follows.

COLLAR: Rnd 1: Sc in BL of each sc around = 14 sc.

Rnd 2 (edging): Sc in FL of next sc, dc in FL of each rem sc to last sc; sc in FL of last sc, changing to black for coat.

COAT: Rnd 1: Hold collar edging back toward you and work sc in unused lp of each sc (behind edging) around = 14 sc. [*NOTE: Leave collar edging facing up toward head*].

Rnds 2 through 24: Rep Rnds 2 through 24 of *Coat instructions for Lady.* At end of Rnd 24, do not join with a sl st in beg sc.

Rnds 25 and 26: Sc in BL of each sc around.

Rnd 27 (edging): Sc in BL of next 2 sc; ch 2, turn. Working in the opposite direction in BL of each st, hdc in each of 2 sc just made, dc in each rem sc around, ending at ch-2; then work dc in unused lp above ch-2 and 5 dc in next unused lp to the left. Continue edging up front center of coat and around neck as follows. Hold work with head to your left and last st worked to your right. * Insert hook from right to left under front (unused) lp of st in next rnd (directly to the left of last st worked) and work one dc; rep from * across center front, ending by working 2 dc in last rnd of black. Continue edging around neck; with head toward you, work to your left in last rnd of black as follows. Work dc in unused lp of each sc around neck, ending by working 2 dc in last st before center edging. Finish off; fold neck edging down away from head and weave end into front center edging.

BASE: Hold bottom edge of coat across top with bottom edging back toward you. Join black with a sl st in unused (back) lp of back center sc (behind edging).

Rnd 1: Working in unused lp of each sc (behind edging), ch 1, sc in same st as joining and in each rem sc around = 47 sc.

Rnd 2: Sc in BL of each sc around = 47 sc.

Rnds 3 through 7: Rep Rnds 8 through 12 of *Dress Trim and Base instructions for Lady Caroler.* [*NOTE: Bottom edging should be facing straight down toward bottom edge.*]

SLEEVE AND HAND (*make 2*): With black, work same as Lady Caroler to Rnd 10. Do not change to lime green in last sc of Rnd 9; continue with black.

Rnd 10: Sc in both lps of each sc around; join with a sl st in both lps of beg sc.

Rnd 11 (edging): Working in both lps of each sc, ch 1, hdc in same sc as joining; dc in each sc around to last sc; sc in last sc, join with a sl st in both lps of beg hdc. Finish off; weave in ends.

Hand: Work same as Lady Caroler.

TOP HAT AND HAIR: With black, ch 4, join with a sl st to form a ring.

Rnd 1: Work 2 sc in each ch around = 8 sc.

Rnd 2: Work 2 sc in BL of each sc around = 16 sc.

Rnd 3: Working in BL of each sc, * 2 sc in each of next 3 sc, sc in next sc; rep from * around = 28 sc.

Rnds 4 through 12: Sc in BL of each sc around.

Rnd 13 (marking rnd): Sc in FL in each of next 18 sc; in next sc, work sc in FL and mark BL for working hair later; sc in FL in each of rem 9 sc. [*NOTE: Back lps are used later for working hair.*]

Rnd 14 (brim): Working in both lps of each sc, * 2 dc in next sc, dc in next sc; rep from * to last 2 sc; 2 dc in next sc, (hdc, sc) in last sc; join with a sl st in both lps of beg dc. Finish off; weave in ends.

Hair: Fold brim edge back toward you until rnd with marked lp is around top. Join dk brown with a sl st in marked lp, ch 1. Working in unused lp of sts in same rnd as marked lp, work loop stitch (see **Fig 3**) in marked lp and in each of next 19 sts (rem 8 sts are left unworked). [*NOTE: Each loop should measure approx 1″in length.*] Finish off, leaving approx 12″ sewing length. Thread into tapestry needle; slip stitch top edge of loop stitches to inside of hat. Leaving brim folded up, except for front of hat, place hat with attached hair on head. Tack in place, if desired.

SCARF: With red, ch 50. Dc in 4th ch from hook and in each of next 8 chs; hdc in each rem ch to last 10 chs; dc in each of last 10 chs. Finish off; weave in ends. Tie scarf around neck between collar and coat edging, having ends at center front. Insert pearl-head straight pin into overlapped ends of scarf at front of neck for stick pin.

Finishing

Facial Features: Trace outlines in **Fig 5** on paper.

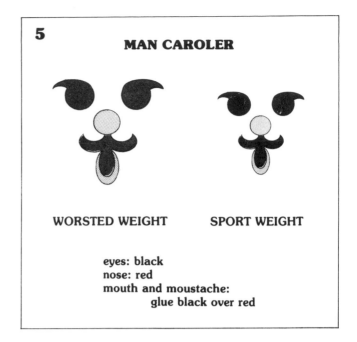

5

MAN CAROLER

WORSTED WEIGHT   SPORT WEIGHT

eyes: black
nose: red
mouth and moustache:
      glue black over red

Cut outlines and use as patterns on felt as indicated. With glue, attach felt pieces as shown in photo.

Place songsheet in arms.

DOG HOWLER

Before proceeding, read General Instructions.

HEAD: With lt brown, ch 4, join with a sl st to form a ring.

Rnd 1: Work 2 sc in each ch around = 8 sc.

Rnd 2: Working in BL of each sc, 2 sc in next sc; pull up lp on hook to 1″, remove hook from lp (do not cut lt brown) and work nose as follows. Leaving 2″end, join black with a sl st in same st as last sc, ch 1, 3 hdc in same st; drop lp from hook; insert hook in first hdc of 3-hdc group just made, hook dropped black lp and pull through; finish off black, leaving 2″ end. Tie black ends tog behind nose just made, leaving ends to inside of work [nose made]. Insert hook in dropped lt brown loop and pull lp taut on hook. Working behind nose, 2 sc in BL of each rem sc = 16 sc.

Rnds 3, 4 and 5: Sc in BL of each sc around.

Rnd 6: Working in BL of each sc, 2 sc in each of next 4 sc, sc in each rem sc around = 20 sc.

Rnd 7: Sc in BL in each of next 2 sc. Work ear as follows: ch 5, 2 tr in 4th ch from hook, (2 dc, sc) in last ch = ear made. Working in BL of each rem sc,

sc in next sc, 2 sc in each of next 2 sc; work ear same as other ear; sc in each rem sc around = 22 sc.

Rnd 8: Working in BL of each sc and keeping ears to front (work behind ears), sc in each sc around = 22 sc.

Rnd 9: Sc in BL of each sc around.

Rnd 10: Working in BL of each sc, sc in each of next 2 sc; * sk one sc, sc in each of next 3 sc; rep from * around = 17 sc.

Rnd 11: Working in BL of each sc, sc in next sc; * sk one sc, sc in each of next 3 sc; rep from * around = 13 sc.

Rnds 12 and 13: Sc in BL of each sc around. Before working next rnd of body, stuff and shape head into a thin oval shape.

BODY: Rnd 1: Working in BL of each sc, sc in next sc; * 2 sc in next sc, sc in each of next 2 sc; rep from * around = 17 sc.

Rnd 2: Working in BL of each sc, sc in each of next 2 sc; * 2 sc in next sc, sc in each of next 2 sc; rep from * around = 22 sc.

Rnd 3 (marking rnd): [*NOTE: In this rnd, 4 sts are marked for sewing front legs to body later*]. Working in BL of each sc, (sc in each of next 2 sc, 2 sc in next sc) 3 times; sc in next sc, 2 sc in next sc; in next sc, work sc in BL and mark FL; sc in next sc, 2 sc in next sc; in next sc, work sc in BL and mark FL; sc in next sc; in next sc, work sc in BL and mark FL; sc in next sc, 2 sc in next sc; in next sc, work sc in BL and mark FL; sc in each of last 2 sc = 28 sc.

Rnds 4 through 9: Sc in BL of each sc around.

Rnd 10 (marking rnd): [*NOTE: In this rnd, 4 sts are marked for sewing hind legs to body later.*] Working in BL of each sc, sc in next sc, (sk one sc, sc in each of next 3 sc) 3 times; sk one sc, sc in each of next 2 sc; in next sc, work sc in BL and mark FL; sk one sc, sc in next sc; in next sc, work sc in BL and mark FL; sc in next sc, sk one sc; in next sc, work sc in BL and mark FL; sc in each of next 2 sc; in next sc, work sc in BL and mark FL; sc in each of last 2 sc = 22 sc.

Rnd 11: Working in BL of each sc, sc in next sc; * sk one sc, sc in each of next 2 sc; rep from * around = 15 sc. Before working next rnd, lightly stuff and shape body into a full oval shape.

Rnd 12: Sc in BL of next sc; * sk one sc, sc in BL of next sc; rep from * around = 8 sc.

Rnd 13: * Sk one sc, sl st in BL of next sc; rep from * around = 4 sl sts. Do not finish off; work tail as follows.

Tail: Ch 1, work 5 dc in last sl st worked, join with a sl st in top of first dc of 5-dc group just made to form a ring. Finish off, leaving 6″ end. Thread into tapestry needle and sew side of tail closed; then secure to end of body.

FRONT LEGS (*make 2*): With lt brown, leave approx 10″ length for sewing to body later, ch 8; join with a sl st to form a ring.

Rnd 1: Sc in each ch around = 8 sc.

Rnds 2 through 5: Sc in both lps of each sc around.

Rnd 6: Working in both lps of each sc, sc in each of next 4 sc, 2 sc in each of rem 4 sc (for front of paw) = 12 sc.

Rnd 7: Sc in both lps of each sc around.

Rnd 8: * Sk next sc, sc in both lps of next sc; rep from * around = 6 sc. Finish off, leaving approx 6″ end. Thread into tapestry needle; weave through sts of last rnd. Draw up tightly and fasten securely. Lightly stuff leg, shaping paw at end (push stuffing down with blunt end of a pencil). Sew beg open edge closed, carefully matching 4 corresponding sc across. Then sew this edge to body between one set of markers below neck.

HIND LEGS (make 2): With lt brown, leave approx 10″ length for sewing to body later, ch 8; join with a sl st to form a ring.

Rnd 1: Sc in each ch around = 8 sc.

Rnd 2: Sc in both lps of each sc around.

Rnd 3: * Sc in both lps of next sc, sk one sc; rep from * around = 4 sc. Finish off, leaving approx 6″ end. Thread into tapestry needle; weave through sts of last rnd. Draw up tightly and fasten securely. Lightly stuff leg. Sew beg open edge closed, carefully matching 4 corresponding sc across. Then sew this edge to body between one set of markers near tail. Continue with same sewing length, tack to middle of front leg.

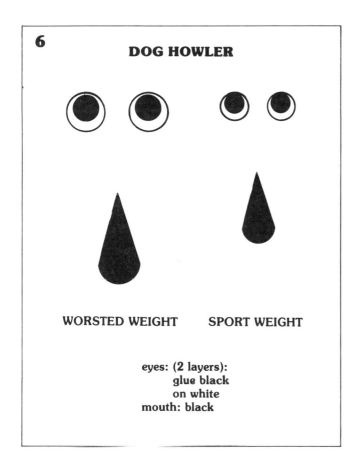

6

DOG HOWLER

WORSTED WEIGHT   **SPORT WEIGHT**

eyes: (2 layers):
glue black
on white
mouth: black

Finishing

Facial Features: Trace outlines in *Fig 6* on paper. Cut outlines and use as patterns on felt as indicated. With glue, attach felt pieces as shown in photo.

Bow: With red, make a chain to measure approx 9″ long. Finish off; knot and trim each end of chain. Place chain around neck and tie into a bow at back.

LAMP POST AND WREATH

Before proceeding, read General Instructions.

TOP: With black, ch 4, join with a sl st to form a ring.

Rnd 1: Work 2 sc in each ch around = 8 sc.

Rnd 2: * Work 3 sc in BL of next sc, sc in BL of next sc; rep from * around = 16 sc.

Rnd 3: Sc in BL of each sc around.

Rnd 4: Working in BL of each sc, sc in next sc; * 3

sc in next sc, sc in each of next 3 sc; rep from * twice more; 3 sc in next sc, sc in each of rem 2 sc = 24 sc.

Rnd 5: Rep Rnd 3.

Rnd 6: Working in BL of each sc, sc in each of next 2 sc; * 3 sc in next sc, sc in each of next 5 sc; rep from * twice more; 3 sc in next sc, sc in each of rem 3 sc = 32 sc.

Rnd 7: Rep Rnd 3.

Rnd 8: Working in BL of each sc, sc in each of next 3 sc; * 3 sc in next sc, sc in each of next 7 sc; rep from * twice more; 3 sc in next sc, sc in each of rem 4 sc = 40 sc.

Rnd 9 (rim): Sc in FL in each of next 3 sc; in next sc, work sc in FL and mark BL (use marker different from beg of rnd) for beg of next rnd; * work (sl st, ch 3, sl st) all in FL of next sc for corner point, sc in FL in each of next 9 sc; rep from * twice more; work (sl st, ch 3, sl st) all in FL of next sc for last corner point, sc in FL in each of next 4 sc, sl st in FL of last sc. Finish off; weave in end.

LAMP: Rnd 1: Hold last rnd (rim) back toward you; join bright yellow with a sl st in marked lp, ch 1. Working in unused lp of each sc in same rnd as marked lp, sc in marked lp; * sk one st, sc in each of next 9 sts; rep from * 3 times more, ending last rep by working sc in each of next 8 sts instead of 9 sts = 36 sc.

Rnd 2: Working in BL of each sc, * dec (decrease) over next 2 sc [**To Dec: Draw up a lp in each of next 2 sc, YO and draw through all 3 lps on hook = dec made**], sc in each of next 7 sc; rep from * 3 times more = 32 sc.

Rnd 3: Sc in BL of each sc around.

Rnd 4: Working in BL of each sc, * dec over next 2 sc, sc in each of next 6 sc; rep from * 3 times more = 28 sc.

Rnd 5: Rep Rnd 3.

Rnd 6: Working in BL of each sc, * dec over next 2 sc, sc in each of next 5 sc; rep from * 3 times more = 24 sc.

Rnd 7: Rep Rnd 3.

Rnd 8: Working in BL of each sc, * dec over next 2 sc, sc in each of next 4 sc; rep from * twice more; dec over next 2 sc, sc in each of next 3 sc; sl st in last sc, changing to black as follows. Insert hook in st, finish off bright yellow; with black, YO and draw through lp on hook. Lightly stuff and shape top and lamp. Continue with black and work post as follows.

POST: Rnd 1: * Working in both lps of each st, dec over next 2 sc; pull up lp on hook to 1", remove hook from lp (do not cut yarn) and work ornamental corner lamp edge as follows. Leaving 2" end for weaving in later, join another strand of black in both lps of decrease st just made, ch 1. Hold work with lamp to your left and last st just worked to your right. Insert hook from right to left under unused (front) lp of st in next bright yellow rnd directly to the left of last st worked and work one sl st loosely. Continue to work sl sts in this manner to corner point of black rim. Finish off; weave in ends [ornamental corner lamp edge made]. Return to working rnd; insert hook in dropped lp and pull lp taut on hook. Sc in both lps in each of next 3 sc; rep from * 3 times more = 16 sc.

Rnd 2: Sc in both lps of each sc around = 16 sc. Rep Rnd 2 until post measures approx 7" for sport weight yarn or 9" for worsted weight yarn (1" less than length of styrofoam rod). Continue with black and work base as follows.

BASE: Rnd 1: * Sc in both lps of next sc, 2 sc in both lps of next sc; rep from * around = 24 sc.

Rnd 2: Sc in both lps of each sc around.

Rnd 3: * Sc in FL in each of next 2 sc, 2 sc in FL of next sc; rep from * around = 32 sc.

Rnd 4: Place metal ring (2" for sport weight yarn or 2½" for worsted weight yarn) on top of rnd and work following sts over it [yarn is kept on top of ring and hook is inserted under ring and into st]. Sc in both lps of each sc around, join with a sl st in both lps of beg sc. Do not finish off; ch 3 and work following rnds for bottom closure.

Rnd 5: Hold last 2 rnds with metal ring back toward you; work sc in unused (back) lp of each sc around = 24 sc. Before working next rnd, insert styrofoam rod (8" length for sport weight yarn or 10" length for worsted weight yarn).

Rnd 6: * Sc in BL of next sc, sk one sc; rep from * around = 12 sc.

Rnd 7: Rep Rnd 6 = 6 sc. Finish off, leaving approx 6" end. Thread into tapestry needle; weave through sts of last rnd. Draw up tightly and fasten securely.

WREATH: With med green, ch 8, join with a sl st to form a rng.

Rnd 1: Ch 3, work 23 dc in ring; join with a sl st in top of beg ch-3.

Rnd 2: Ch 1, sc in same st as joining; * ch 3, work (sc, ch 3, sc) all in next dc; ch 3, sc in next dc; rep from * to last dc; ch 3, (sc, ch 3, sc) all in last dc, ch 3; join with a sl st in beg sc. Finish off, weave in ends.

Bow: With red, ch 40. Finish off; weave in ends. Slip chain around ch-3 of first rnd of wreath and tie into a bow.

Berries: With red sewing thread, attach two groups of 3 red beads each to wreath as shown in photo. Attach wreath to post with green yarn as positioned in photo.

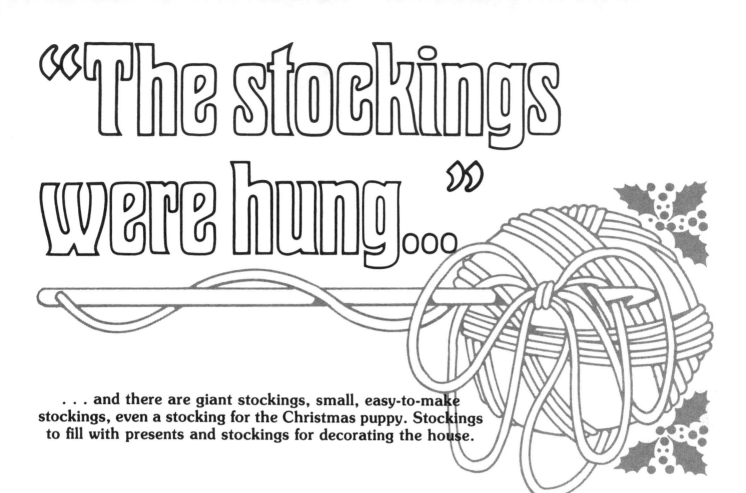

"The stockings were hung..."

... and there are giant stockings, small, easy-to-make stockings, even a stocking for the Christmas puppy. Stockings to fill with presents and stockings for decorating the house.

PUPPY DOG STOCKING

designed by Sue Penrod

Your favorite dog can be included in the holiday festivities with its own stocking filled with dog biscuits and chewy toys.

Size

Approx 10½" long

Materials

American Thread Dawn Sayelle Knitting Worsted Size Yarn:
    3½ oz Shaded Beiges
    1 oz Copper
    ¼ oz each of Flame and Black
Size I aluminum crochet hook (or size required for gauge)
Small pieces of felt in white, tan, red and black.
Tracing paper and pencil
White craft glue

Gauge

In sc, 7 sts = 2"; 4 rnds = 1"

Instructions

Beg at toe, with Shaded Beiges, ch 4, join with a sl st to form a ring.

Rnd 1: Work 2 sc in each ch around = 8 sc. Do not join; work continuous rnds, unless otherwise specified. Use small safety pin or piece of yarn in contrasting color and mark first st of rnd; move marker at beg of each rnd.

Rnd 2: Work 2 sc in each sc around = 16 sc.

Rnd 3: Rep Rnd 2 = 32 sc.

Rnd 4: Work even. (*Work sc in each st around, without increasing or decreasing.*)

Rnd 5: * Sc in each of next 3 sc, 2 sc in next sc; rep from * around = 40 sc.

Rnds 6 through 13: Work 8 rnds even.

Rnd 14: Ch 20, sk first 20 sc (*for working back of stocking later*), sc in each of rem 20 sc.

Rnd 15: Sc in each of 20 chs, sc in each of next 20 sc = 40 sc.

Rnd 16: Work even.

Rnd 17: * Sc in each of next 2 sc, sk one sc, sc in next sc; rep from * around = 30 sc.

Rnd 18: Work even.

Rnd 19: *Sc in next sc, sk one sc, sc in next sc; rep from * around = 20 sc.

Rnd 20: Work even.

Rnd 21: * Sc in next sc, sk one sc; rep from * around = 10 sc.

Rnds 22 through 25 (tail): Work 4 rnds even.

Rnd 26: * Sl st in next sc, sk one sc; rep from * around = 5 sl sts. Finish off, leaving approx 6″ end. Thread into tapestry or yarn needle. Weave through sts of last rnd; draw up tightly and fasten securely on inside.

BODY AND HEAD: Hold work with tail facing you and open edge across top. Join Shaded Beiges with a sl st in unused lp of first ch to your right.

Rnd 1: Ch 1, sc in same st as joining and in each of next 19 chs; sc in next row, sc in each of next 20 sc across front, sc in next row = 42 sc. Do not join; work continuous rnds (*remember to mark first st of rnd*).

Rnds 2 through 10: Work 9 rnds even.

Rnd 11 (marking rnd): Sc in first sc and mark this st for sewing front leg to body later (*use marker different from beg of rnd*). Sc in each of next 20 sc, sc in next sc and mark this st for sewing other front leg to body later, sc in each of rem 20 sc.

Rnds 12 through 15: Work 4 rnds even.

Rnd 16 (beading rnd): * Sc in next sc, ch 1, sk one sc; rep from * around.

Rnd 17: Sc in each sc and in each ch-1 sp around = 42 sc.

Rnds 18 through 30: Work 13 rnds even.

Rnd 31 (ears): Sc in each of next 2 sc, * sc **in back lp** (*lp away from you*) in each of next 6 sc. Pull up lp on hook to approx 2″; remove hook from lp (do not cut yarn) and work ear as follows: Turn work around until top of sts just worked are facing you.

> **Row 1:** With Copper, make a slip knot on hook; join with a sc **in front lp** of st where last sc was worked; sc **in front lp** in each of next 5 sts = 6 sc.
>
> **Row 2:** Ch 1, turn; sc in each of first 2 sc, 2 sc in next sc, sc in each of rem 3 sc = 7 sc.
>
> **Row 3:** Ch 1, turn; sc in each of first 3 sc, 2 sc in next sc, sc in each rem sc = 8 sc.

Row 4: Rep Row 3 = 9 sc.

Row 5: Ch 1, turn; sc in each of first 4 sc, 2 sc in next sc, sc in each rem sc = 10 sc.

Row 6: Rep Row 5 = 11 sc.

Row 7: Ch 1, turn; sc in each of first 5 sc, 2 sc in next sc, sc in each of rem 5 sc = 12 sc. Finish off; weave in ends. *

One ear is now completed. Turn work around and continue with working rnd as follows: Sc **in both lps** in each of next 18 sc, rep from * to * once (for other ear), sc **in both lps** in each of rem 10 sc.

(*NOTE: Continue by working in both lps of sts.*)

Rnd 32: Work even.

Rnd 33: Sc in each of first 17 sc, work (sc, ch 8, sc) in next sc for hanger, sc in each of next 10 sc, sl st in next sc. Finish off (*leaving rem sts unworked*); weave in ends.

FRONT LEGS (*worked in one piece*): With Shaded Beiges, leave approx 12″ end for sewing leg to body later, ch 4, join with a sl st to form a ring.

Rnd 1: Work 2 sc in each ch around = 8 sc. Do not join; work continuous rnds (*mark first st of rnd*).

Rnd 2: Work 2 sc in each sc around = 16 sc.

Rnds 3 through 15: Work 13 rnds even.

Rnd 16: * Sc in next sc, sk one sc; rep from * around = 8 sc.

Rnd 17: Rep Rnd 16 = 4 sc. One leg is now completed; continue with other leg as follows:

Rnd 18: Work 2 sc in each sc around = 8 sc.

Rnds 19 through 34: Rep Rnds 2 through 17. At end of Rnd 34, finish off, leaving approx 12″ sewing length. Thread into tapestry or yarn needle; sew leg just completed to side of stocking, aligning last rnd at marker. Then sew other leg to opposite side in same manner.

TIE: With Flame, make a chain to measure approx 24″ long. Finish off; knot and trim each end of chain. Beg and ending at side, weave chain through sps of beading rnd. Tie ends into a bow.

MUZZLE: With Copper, make two 1½″ diameter pompons (see instructions on page 11). Attach pompons side by side to center front of stocking, just above tie. For nose, make ¾″ diameter Black pompon and attach between and at top of other pompons.

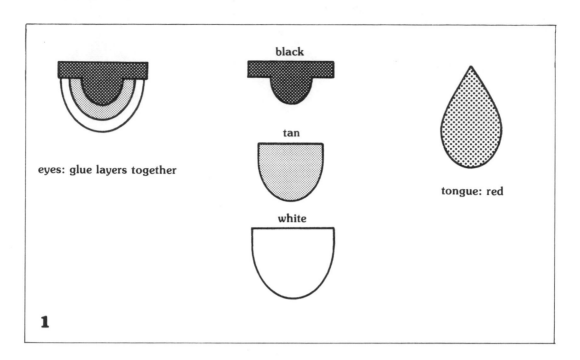

eyes: glue layers together

black

tan

white

tongue: red

1

EYES AND TONGUE: Trace outlines in *Fig 1* on paper. Cut outlines and use as patterns on felt as indicated. (*NOTE: To prevent pattern piece from slipping on felt, tape piece in place with cellophane tape. Cut felt through tape; then discard tape.*) With glue, attach felt pieces as shown in photo.

Green version   Red version

GIANT RIBBED CHRISTMAS STOCKINGS

These colorful, giant stockings will hold a lot of wonderful surprises! We've made up two versions of the same basic pattern, one with a lacy cuff, one more tailored. Trim them with yarn laces or pompons.

Size

Approx 6½″ wide x 18″ long

Materials

American Thread Dawn Sayelle Knitting Worsted Size Yarn:

   For Red Stocking
      6 oz Flame
      1 oz each of White and Golf Green
   For Green Stocking
      6 oz Golf Green
      2 oz White

Sizes J and K aluminum crochet hooks (or size required for gauge)

Gauge

With smaller size hook in FP Patt, 4 sts = 1¼″; 2 rows = 1″

Pattern Stitch

FRONT POST *(abbreviated FP).* To make a practice swatch, first ch 14. *(NOTE: This is worked on an odd number of sts.)*

Row 1 (right side): Sc in 2nd ch from hook and in each rem ch across.

Row 2: Ch 1, turn; sc in each sc across.

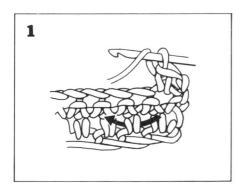

Row 3: Ch 1, turn; sc in first sc, work FPdc *(front post dc)* around post of 2nd sc in 2nd row below as follows: YO, insert hook *from front to back to front* around post of st *(Fig 1)*; hook yarn and draw lp through; complete st as a dc = FPdc made. * Return to working row; sk next sc *(behind FPdc just made)*, sc in next sc. Return to 2nd row below; sk one sc from prev FPdc, work FPdc around post of next sc. Rep from * last sc; sc in last sc.

Row 4: Ch 1, turn; sc in first sc, * sc in FPdc, sc in next sc; rep from * across.

Row 5: Ch 1, turn; sc in first sc, work FPdc around post of first FPdc in 2nd row below. * Return to working row; sk next sc *(behind FPdc just made)*; sc in next sc. Return to 2nd row below; work FPdc around post of next FPdc. Rep from * to last sc; sc in last sc. Rep Rows 4 and 5 for patt.

Instructions

Beg at top, with smaller size hook and Flame or Golf Green, ch 42. Work in FP Patt St on 41 sts until piece measures approx 10″ long. Continuing in FP Patt St, work heel shaping as follows.

SHAPE HEEL: *(NOTE: Shaping is worked in short rows. When instructions say "turn", leave rem sts unworked; turn work and begin next row.)*

First Half: Row 1: Work in FP Patt St across first 7 sc.

Row 2: Turn; sk first sc, * sc in FPdc, sc in next sc; rep from * across = 6 sc.

Row 3: Work in FP Patt St across the following sts: 6 sc of prev row, skipped sc, and next 2 sc (left unworked in Row 1) = 9 sts.

Row 4: Rep Row 2 = 8 sc.

Row 5: Work in FP Patt St across the following sts: scs of prev row, skipped sc, and next 2 sc (left unworked in Row 1) = 11 sts.

Rows 6 through 14: Rep Rows 4 and 5, 4 times; then rep Row 4 once more. *(NOTE: You will be adding 2 sts every 2 rows.)* At end of Row 14, you should have 18 sc.

Row 15: Work in FP Patt St across the following sts: 18 sc of prev row, skipped sc, and rem 22 sc *(left unworked in Row 1)* = 41 sc. First half of heel shaping is now completed. Mark last st worked *(use small safety pin or piece of yarn in contrasting color)* for measurement later. Continue with 2nd half.

Second Half: Row 1: Ch 1, turn; sc in each of first 7 sts.

Row 2: Turn; sk first sc, * work FPdc around post of FPdc in 2nd row below. Return to working row; sk sc *(behind FPdc just made)*, sc in next sc. Rep from * across = 6 sts.

Row 3: Ch 1, turn; sc in each st of prev row, sc in skipped sc, sc in each of next 2 sts = 9 sc.

Rows 4 through 14: Rep Rows 2 and 3, 5 times; then rep Row 2 once more. At end of Row 14, you should have 18 sts.

Row 15: Ch 1, turn; sc in each of 18 sts of prev row, sc in skipped sc, sc in each of rem 22 sts = 41 sc. Heel shaping is now completed; continue with foot shaping.

FOOT SHAPING: Continuing in FP Patt St, work even until piece measures approx 8″ from marker *(measure along outside edge)*, ending by working Row 3 (sc row). Now shape toe as follows.

Row 1: Ch 1, turn; dec (decrease) over first 2 sc **(To work dec: Draw up a lp in each of 2 sts, YO and draw through all 3 lps on hook = dec made)**; sc in each of next 16 sc, dec, sc in next sc, dec; sc in each of next 16 sc, dec over last 2 sc = 37 sts.

Row 2: Ch 1, turn; sc in each st across.

Row 3: Ch 1, turn; dec, sc in each of next 14 sc; dec, sc in next sc, dec; sc in each of next 14 sc, dec = 33 sts.

Row 4: Rep Row 2.

Row 5: Ch 1, turn; dec, sc in each of next 12 sc; dec, sc in next sc, dec; sc in each of next 12 sc, dec = 29 sts.

Row 6: Rep Row 2.

Row 7: Ch 1, turn; (dec) twice, sc in each of next 6

sc; (dec) twice, sc in next sc, (dec) twice; sc in each of next 6 sc, (dec) twice = 21 sts.

Row 8: Rep Row 2.

Row 9: Ch 1, turn; (dec) twice, sc in each of next 2 sc; (dec) twice, sc in next sc, (dec) twice; sc in each of next 2 sc, (dec) twice = 13 sts.

Row 10: Rep Row 2. Finish off, leaving approx 24″ sewing length. Thread into tapestry or yarn needle. Weave through sts of last row; draw up tightly and fasten securely on inside. Then sew side seam.

Finishing Red Stocking

CUFF: (*NOTE: All rnds are worked on right side.*) With larger size hook and White, ch 42 loosely; join with a sl st in beg ch to form a ring (*be careful not to twist chain*).

Rnd 1: Ch 1, sc in same ch as joining and in each rem ch around; join with a sl st in beg sc = 42 sc.

Rnd 2: Ch 1, sc in same st as joining and in each rem sc around; join with a sl st in beg sc, changing to Golf Green [**To change colors: Drop color being used (do not cut—will be used later); insert hook in beg sc, hook new color (leave approx 3″ end for weaving in now or later) and draw through st and lp on hook = color changed.**]

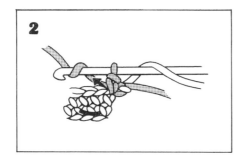

Rnd 3: With Golf Green, ch 1, sc in same st as joining; dc in next sc in 2nd row below (*Fig 2*); * sc in next sc, dc in next sc in 2nd row below; rep from * around, join with a sl st in beg sc.

Rnd 4: Continuing with Golf Green, ch 1, sc in same st as joining and in each rem st around; join with a sl st in beg sc, changing to White. (*Drop Golf Green—do not cut; pick up White from behind work.*)

Rnd 5: With White, ch 1, dc in first sc in 2nd row below, sc in next sc; * dc in next sc in 2nd row below, sc in next sc; rep from * around, join with a sl st in beg dc.

Rnd 6: Continuing with White, ch 1, sc in same st as joining and in each rem st around; join with a sl st in beg sc, changing to Golf Green.

Rnds 7 through 9: Rep Rnds 3 through 5.

Rnd 10 (joining cuff and stocking): Continue with White; finish off Golf Green. Slip cuff over stocking, having right side of each piece facing you, and with joining of rnds on cuff aligned with seam on stocking. Carefully matching sts around top edge on both pieces (*match extra st on cuff with seam on stocking*), join pieces tog as follows: Ch 1, sc in same st as joining and in each rem st around. Join another strand of White and work hanger as follows: In beg sc of rnd, work (sl st, ch 18, sl st). Finish off; weave in ends.

POMPONS: Following instructions on page 11, use equal amounts of White and Golf Green and make three 1½″ diameter pompons. Sew pompons evenly spaced down front of stocking as shown in photo.

Finishing Green Stocking

CUFF: (*NOTE: All rnds are worked on right side.*) With larger size hook and White, ch 42 loosely; join with a sl st in beg ch to form a ring (*be careful not to twist chain*).

Rnd 1: Ch 1, sc in same ch as joining and in each rem ch around; join with a sl st in beg sc = 42 sc.

Rnd 2: Ch 1, sc in same st as joining and in each rem sc around; join with a sl st **in front lp** of beg sc.

Rnd 3 (ruffle): **Working in front lp of each st around,** ch 1, work (sc, ch 3, sc) in same st as joining; * ch 3, sc in next st, ch 3, work (sc, ch 3, sc) in next st; rep from * to last st, ch 3, sc in last st. Do not join.

Rnd 4: **Working in back lp of each st around (behind ruffle),** sc in each st around; join with a sl st in both lps of beg sc. **Continue by working in both lps of sts.**

Rnds 5 through 13: Rep Rnds 2 through 4, 3 times.

Rnd 14 (joining cuff and stocking): Slip cuff over stocking, having right side of each piece facing you, and with joining of rnds on cuff aligned with seam on stocking. Carefully matching sts around top edge of both pieces (*match extra st on cuff with seam on stocking*), join pieces tog as follows: Ch 1, sc in same st as joining and in each rem st around. Join another strand of White and work hanger as follows: In beg sc of rnd, work (sl st, ch 18, sl st). Finish off; weave in ends.

LACE: With smaller size hook and 2 strands of White, make a chain to measure approx 36″ long. Finish off; knot and trim each end of chain. Beg at ankle and lace chain up center front of stocking, passing chain under FP sts on each side of center 2 FP sts, every 3rd row.

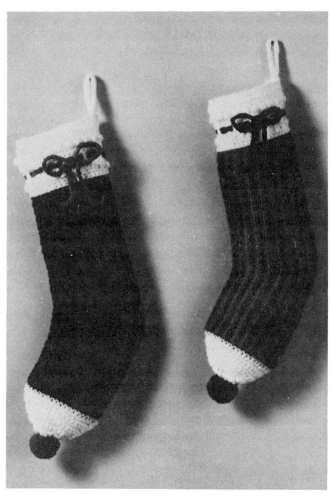

SANTA SOCK

designed by Louise O'Donnell and Mary Thomas

Here's a Christmas stocking worked in one piece and sized just right for making quickly—each family member can have his very own! The stocking also makes a delightful "package" into which to tuck an inexpensive gift for a friend.

Size

Approx 5" wide x 15" long

Materials

Sport weight yarn:
   For Version A
   2 oz red
   ½ oz white
   ¼ oz green
   For Version B
   2 oz green
   ½ oz white
   ¼ oz red
Aluminum crochet hook size H (or size required for gauge) for both versions

Gauge

In sc, 4 sts = 1"; 5 rows = 1"

Pattern Stitch

FRONT POST (abbreviated FP). To practice stitch, first work 2 rows even in sc. (*NOTE: This is worked on uneven number of sts.*)

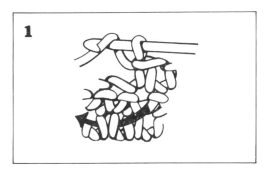

Foundation Row (right side): Ch 1, turn; sc in first sc, work FP around post of 2nd sc in 2nd row below (*Fig 1*) [**To make FP: YO, insert hook from front to back to front around post of st; draw lp through and complete st as a dc = FP made**]. * † Return to working row: sk next sc (*behind FP just made*), sc in next sc †. Return to 2nd row below: sk one sc from last FP, FP around post of next sc; rep from * across to last 2 sc, rep from † to †.

Row 1: Ch 1, turn; sc in first sc, * sc in FP, sc in next sc; rep from * across.

Row 2: Ch 1, turn; sc in first sc, FP around post of first FP in 2nd row below. * † Return to working row: sk next sc (behind FP), sc in next sc †. Return to 2nd row below: FP around post of next FP; rep from * across to last 2 sc, rep from † to †. Rep Rows 1 and 2 for patt.

Instructions

Beg at top with white, ch 42. (*NOTE: Instructions are the same for both versions; use color in brackets when making Version B.*)

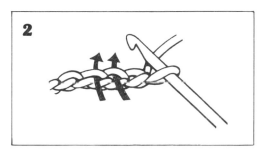

Row 1 (right side): Sc in back ridge (*Fig 2*) of 2nd ch from hook and in each rem ch across = 41 sc.

Row 2: Ch 1, turn; sc in **front lp only** (lp toward you) of each sc across.

Row 3: Ch 1, turn; sc in **back lp only** (lp away from you) of each sc across.

Row 4: Rep Row 2.

Continue by working in **both lps** of sts.

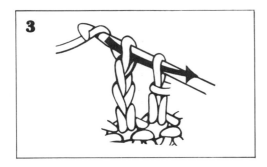

Row 5: Ch 1, turn; sc in first sc, * work blackberry st (abbreviated BB) in next sc [to make **BB**: draw up a lp in sc (2 lps now on hook); using last lp on hook, ch 3; keeping ch-3 just made to front of work, YO and draw through both lps on hook (**Fig 3**) = BB made]; sc in next sc; rep from * across.

Row 6: Ch 1, turn; sc in each st across = 41 sc.

Row 7 (beading row): Ch 4, turn; sk first 2 sc, dc in next sc; * ch 1, sk one sc, dc in next sc; rep from * across.

Row 8: Ch 1, turn; sc in first dc, * in ch-1 sp, sc in next dc; rep from * across, ending sc in Tch sp, sc in 3rd ch of Tch = 41 sc.

Row 9: Rep Row 5.

Row 10: Rep Row 2, changing to red [green] in last sc [**To change colors: Work st until 2 lps rem on hook, finish off color just used; hook new color leaving 4″ end and draw through 2 lps on hook = color change made**].

Row 11: Continuing with red [green], rep Row 3.

Row 12: Rep Row 6.

Row 13: Work Foundation Row of FP patt.

Rows 14 through 42: Rep Rows 1 and 2 of FP patt, 14 times; then rep Row 1, once more.

SHAPE HEEL AND FOOT: (*NOTE: Continuing in FP patt, shaping is worked in short rows; when instructions say "turn," leave rem sts unworked; turn work and begin next row.*)

Right Heel Shaping: Row 1: Work in FP patt across first 7 sc. Mark last st worked to be used later in Row 3.

Row 2: Turn; sk first sc, * sc in next FP, sc in next sc; rep from * across = 6 sc.

Row 3: Work in FP patt across the following 9 sts: first 6 sc of prev row, marked sc (where sk sc of prev row was worked), and next 2 sc (left unworked in Row 1).

Row 4: Rep Row 2 = 8 sc.

Row 5: Work in FP patt across the following 11 sts: 8 sc, † st where sk sc of prev row was worked, and next 2 sc (left unworked in Row 1) †.

Row 6: Rep Row 2 = 10 sc.

Row 7: Work in FP patt across the following 13 sts: 10 sc, rep from † to † (in Row 5).

Row 8: Rep Row 2 = 12 sc.

Row 9: Work in FP patt across the following 15 sts: 12 sc, rep from † to †.

Row 10: Rep Row 2 = 14 sc.

Row 11: Work in FP patt across the following 17 sts: 14 sc, rep from † to †.

Row 12: Rep Row 2 = 16 sc.

Row 13: Work in FP patt across the following 19 sts: 16 sc, rep from † to †.

Row 14: Rep Row 2 = 18 sc.

Row 15: Work in FP patt across the following sts of entire row: 18 sc, same sc where sk sc was worked, rem 22 sc = 41 sc.

Left Heel Shaping: Row 1: Ch 1, turn; sc in each of first 7 sts.

Row 2: Turn; sk first sc, * FP around post of FP in 2nd row below. Return to working row: sk sc behind FP, sc in next sc; rep from * across = 6 sts.

Row 3: Ch 1, turn; sc in each of the following 9 sts: first 6 sts of prev row, † sc where sk sc of prev row was worked, and next 2 sts (left unworked in Row 1) †.

Row 4: Rep Row 2 = 8 sts.

Row 5: Ch 1, turn; sc in each of the following 11 sts: first 8 sts, rep from † to † (in Row 3).

Row 6: Rep Row 2 = 10 sts.

Row 7: Ch 1, turn; sc in each of the following 13 sts: first 10 sts, rep from † to †.

Row 8: Rep Row 2 = 12 sts.

Row 9: Ch 1, turn; sc in each of the following 15 sts: first 12 sts, rep from † to †.

Row 10: Rep Row 2 = 14 sts.

Row 11: Ch 1, turn; sc in each of the following 17 sts: first 14 sts, rep from † to †.

Row 12: Rep Row 2 = 16 sts.

Row 13: Ch 1, turn; sc in each of the following 19 sts: first 16 sts, rep from † to †.

Row 14: Rep Row 2 = 18 sts.

Row 15: Ch 1, turn; sc in each of the following sts across entire row: first 18 sts, same sc where sk sc was worked, rem 22 sts = 41 sc.

Foot: Beg with Row 2 of FP patt and work 15 rows even in FP patt, ending by working Row 2. At end of last row, change to white in last sc as before.

Shape Toe: Row 1 (wrong side): Ch 1, turn; sc in each st across.

Row 2: Ch 1, turn; decrease (dec) over first 2 sc [**to dec: Draw up a lp in each of 2 sts, YO and draw through all 3 lps on hook = dec made**]. Sc in each of next 16 sc; dec, sc in next sc, dec; sc in each of next 16 sc, dec = 37 sts.

Row 3: Rep Row 1.

Row 4: Ch 1, turn; dec, sc in each of next 14 sc; dec, sc in next sc, dec; sc in each of next 14 sc, dec = 33 sts.

Row 5: Rep Row 1.

Row 6: Ch 1, turn; dec, sc in each of next 12 sc; dec, sc in next sc, dec; sc in each of next 12 sc, dec = 29 sts.

Row 7: Rep Row 1.

Row 8: Ch 1, turn; dec twice, sc in each of next 6 sc; dec twice, sc in next sc, dec twice; sc in each of next 6 sc, dec twice = 21 sts.

Row 9: Ch 1, turn; dec twice, sc in each of next 2 sc; dec twice, sc in next sc, dec twice; sc in each of next 2 sc, dec twice = 13 sts.

Row 10: Dec 3 times, sc in next sc, dec 3 times = 7 sts. Finish off, leaving approx 14″ sewing length.

Finishing

Thread yarn at end of toe into tapestry needle; weave through sts of last row. Draw up tightly and fasten securely. Then sew toe and side seam using matching yarn.

Hanger: With white, ch 18, hdc in 3rd ch from hook and in each rem ch across. Finish off; fold in half and sew ends to sock at seam.

Tie: With 2 strands of green [red], make a chain to measure approx 26″ or desired length. Weave through beading row (see photo) and tie in a bow. Knot each end of tie.

Pompon: Make 1½″ diameter green [red] pompon (see Pompon instructions on page 11) and sew to end of toe.

"...nestled all snug in their beds"

. . . and what could be better than to "settle down for a long winter's nap" covered with your own delightful afghan, made just for Christmas.

POINSETTIA AFGHAN

designed by Mary Thomas

This striking afghan will brighten up your home for the holidays. Its unusual design is quick and easy to make.

Size

Approx 43″ x 67″

Materials

American Thread Dawn Sayelle Knitting Worsted
   Size Yarn:
      36 oz Golf Green
      12 oz Flame
      4 oz Lemon
Size H aluminum crochet hook (or size required for
   gauge)

Gauge

One motif = 9½″ (measured across from side to side)

Motif Instructions

(**Make 33**): With Lemon, ch 2.

Rnd 1 (right side): Work 6 sc in 2nd ch from hook, join with a sl st in beg sc.

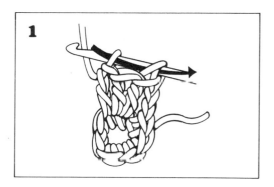

Rnd 2: Do not turn; work beg PC (*popcorn*) as follows: Ch 3, work 3 dc in same sc as joining; drop lp from hook, insert hook in top of ch-3; then hook dropped lp and pull through lp on hook— *Fig 1* (*beg PC made*). * Ch 2, work PC in next sc as follows: Work 4 dc in sc, drop lp from hook; insert hook in first dc of 4-dc group just made, hook dropped lp and pull through lp on hook (PC made); rep from * 4 times more. Ch 2, join with a sl st in top of ch-3 of beg PC = 6 PC. Finish off Lemon.

Rnd 3: [*NOTE: In this rnd, red leaves are worked. Each leaf is worked back and forth in rows, attaching* *base of leaf to ch-2 sp(between PCs)].*With right side facing, join Flame with a sl st in any ch-2 sp.

* **Work leaf as follows: Row 1:** Ch 4, sc in 2nd ch from hook and in each of rem 2 chs; sl st back into same ch-2 sp.

Row 2: Ch 1, turn; sc in each sc across = 3 sc.

Row 3: Ch 4, turn; sc in 2nd ch from hook and in each of next 2 chs, sc in each of next 3 sc; sl st back into same ch-2 sp = 6 sc.

Row 4: Ch 1, turn; sc in each sc across = 6 sc.

Row 5: Ch 4, turn; sc in 2nd ch from hook and in each of next 2 chs. Work picot as follows: Ch 2, sl st in 2nd ch from hook *(picot made)*. Sc in next sc, hdc in each of next 2 sc; work picot as before, dc in each of next 2 sc; picot, work (dc, hdc) in last sc; sl st back into same ch-2 sp. One leaf is now completed. Working behind next PC, sl st into next ch-2 sp. Rep from * 5 times more, ending last rep by working sl st into beg ch-2 sp *(where first leaf was worked)*. Finish off Flame.

Rnd 4: [*NOTE: All following rnds are worked on right side.*] Join Golf Green with a sl st in sc at tip of any leaf. Ch 1, beg in same st as joining and work as follows: * Sc in sc at tip of leaf, ch 4, sc in next picot of same leaf; work (ch 3, sc in next picot of same leaf) twice. Continuing on next leaf, sc at beg of first row, ch 3; sc at beg of 3rd row, ch 4. Rep from * 5 times more, join with a sl st in beg sc.

Rnd 5: Ch 1, beg in same st as joining and work as follows: * Work 3 sc in sc at tip of leaf *(for corner)*; 3 sc in ch-4 sp, hdc in next sc; 2 hdc in ch-3 sp, dc in next sc; work dc dec (decrease) over next ch-3 sp and next sc [**To work dc dec: Work (YO hook, insert hook in next sp/st and draw up a lp, YO and draw through 2 lps on hook) twice; YO and draw through all 3 lps on hook = dc dec made.**] Work dc dec over next sc and ch-3 sp, hdc in next sc, 3 sc in ch-4 sp. Rep from * 5 times more, join with a sl st in beg sc.

Rnd 6: Ch 1, sc in same st as joining. * Work 3 sc in center st at corner; sc in each of next 5 sts, hdc in next st, dc in next st; work (dc dec over next 2 sts) twice; dc in next st, hdc in next st, sc in each of next 2 sts. Rep from * 5 times more, ending last rep by working sc in last st *(instead of sc in each of next 2 sts)*. Join with a sl st in beg sc.

Rnd 7: Ch 1, hdc in same st as joining, hdc in next st. * Work 3 sc in center st at corner; sc in each of next 2 sts, hdc in each of next 4 sts; dc in each of next 2 sts, work dc dec over next 2 sts; dc in each of next 3 sts, hdc in each of next 2 sts. Rep from * 5 times more, ending last rep without working hdc in each of next 2 sts. Join with a sl st in beg hdc.

Rnd 8: Ch 1, hdc in same st as joining, hdc in next st. * Sc in next st, work 3 sc in center st at corner; sc in each of next 5 sts, hdc in each of next 2 sts; dc in each of next 6 sts, hdc in each of next 2 sts. Rep from * 5 times more, ending last rep without working hdc in each of next 2 sts. Join with a sl st in beg hdc.

Rnd 9: Ch 1, sc in same st as joining. * Sc in each st to center st at next corner, work 3 sc in center corner st; rep from * 5 times more. Sc in each rem st, join with a sl st in beg sc. Finish off; weave in ends.

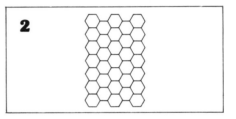

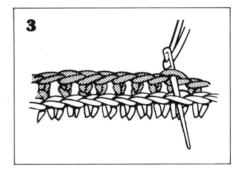

Assembling

Arrange motifs as shown in *Fig 2.* To join, hold 2 motifs with right sides tog. Thread Golf Green into tapestry or yarn needle. Carefully matching corresponding sts across side, beg in center sc at corner and sew with overcast st **in outer lps only** *(Fig 3)* across, ending in center sc at next corner. Continue to join sides of motifs in this manner until all motifs are joined. Weave in all ends. Lightly steam press joinings on wrong side.

SNOW CLUSTERS BABY AFGHAN

designed by Mary Thoms

Make this elegant white afghan for baby to sleep under during the Christmas season.

Size

Approx 34" x 42"

Materials

American Thread Dawn Wintuk Sport Yarn:
    18 oz White
Size H aluminum crochet hook (or size required for gauge)

Gauge

In sc, 17 sts = 4"

Pattern Stitch

PUFF STITCH (abbreviated PS): Work (YO hook, insert hook in st and draw up a lp) 3 times (7 *lps now on hook*); YO and draw through all 7 lps on hook (**Fig 1**), ch 1 = PS made.

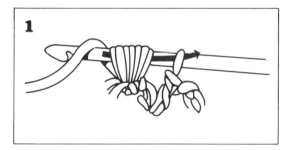

Instructions

Ch 143 loosely.

Row 1 (right side): Sc in 2nd ch from hook and in next ch; * sk one ch, work 3 sc in next ch; sk one ch, sc in each of next 2 chs; rep from * across = 28 3-sc groups.

Row 2: Ch 3, turn; dc in next sc (*do not work in first sc*); * sk one sc, work (PS, ch 1, PS) in next sc (*center sc of 3-sc group*); sk one sc, dc in each of next 2 sc; rep from * across.

Row 3: Ch 1, turn; sc in each of first 2 dc, * work 3 sc in next ch-1 sp (*between pair of PS*), sc in each of next 2 dc; rep from * across, ending last rep by working sc in top of ch-3 = 142 sc.

Rep Rows 2 and 3 until afghan measures approx 42" long, ending by working Row 3. Finish off; weave in all ends.

CHRISTMAS GRANNY

designed by Joan Kokaska

A Christmas afghan made with the traditional granny square brings back warm memories of childhood days. Here's an easy-to-make project that will certainly become a cherished family heirloom, to be unwrapped proudly each holiday season.

Size

Approx 45″ x 63″

Materials

Worsted weight yarn:
    8 oz white
    8 oz Christmas red
    22 oz light green
    16 oz Christmas green

Size G aluminum crochet hook (or size required for gauge)

Gauge

One square = 4½″

SQUARE A (make 84)

Instructions

With Christmas red, ch 5, join with a sl st to form a ring. (*NOTE: All rounds are worked on right side.*)

Rnd 1: Ch 3, 2 dc in ring; (ch 3, 3 dc in ring) 3 times, ch 3; join with a sl st in top of beg ch-3. Finish off. (*NOTE: Ch-3 counts as one dc throughout patt.*)

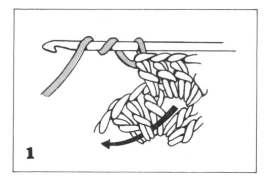

Rnd 2: With right side facing, join white with a sl st in any ch-3 sp; ch 3, (dc, ch 3, 2 dc) in same sp as joining [*beg corner made*]: dc in next dc, tr in base of next dc [**To Work Tr: YO twice, insert hook under 2 threads at base of next dc (*Fig 1*); hook yarn and draw lp through st (4 lps now on hook); (YO and draw through 2 lps on hook) 3 times = tr made**]; dc in next dc [*first side completed*]; * work (2 dc, ch 3, 2 dc) in next ch-3 sp [*next corner made*]; dc in next dc, tr in base of next dc, dc in next dc [*next side made*]; rep from * twice more, join with a sl st in top of beg ch-3. Finish off.

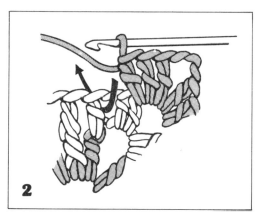

Rnd 3: With right side facing, join Christmas green with a sl st in any ch-3 corner sp; ch 3, work (2 dc, ch 3, 3 dc) in same sp; sk 2 dc, 3 dc in sp *between* sts [*skipped dc and next dc—Fig 2*]; sk next 3 sts [*dc, tr, dc*], 3 dc in sp between sts [*skipped dc and next dc*]; * work (3 dc, ch 3, 3 dc) in next ch-3 corner sp; sk 2 dc, 3 dc in sp between sts [*skipped dc and next dc*]; sk next 3 sts [*dc, tr, dc*], 3 dc in sp between sts [*skipped dc and next dc*]; rep from * twice more, join with a sl st in top of beg ch-3. Finish off.

Rnd 4: With right side facing, join light green with a sl st in any ch-3 corner sp; ch 3, work (dc, ch 3, 2 dc) in same sp; work (dc in next dc, tr in base of next dc, dc in next dc) 4 times; * work (2 dc, ch 3, 2 dc) in next ch-3 corner sp; work (dc in next dc, tr in base of next dc, dc in next dc) 4 times; rep from * twice more, join with a sl st in top of beg ch-3. Finish off; weave in all ends.

SQUARE B (make 56)

Instructions

Following instructions for Square A, beg with white and work rnds in the following color sequence:

Rnd 1: White

Rnd 2: Christmas red

Rnd 3: Christmas green

Rnd 4: Light green

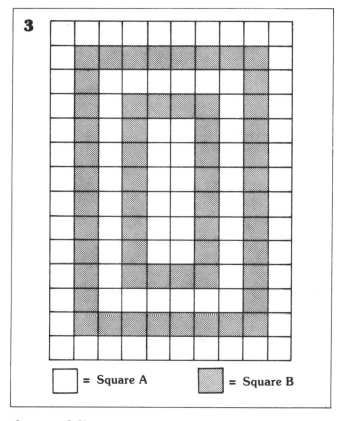

☐ = Square A   ▨ = Square B

Assembling

Position squares as shown in *Fig 3,* having right side of each square facing up. To join, hold two squares with right sides facing. Thread light green into tapestry needle. Carefully matching corresponding sts across side, beg in center ch of corner and sew with overcast st **in outer lps only (*Fig 4*)** across, ending in center ch of next corner. Join squares into rows; then sew rows tog, being sure that all four-corner junctions are firmly joined.

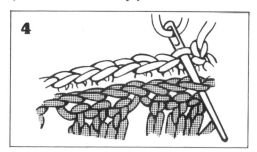

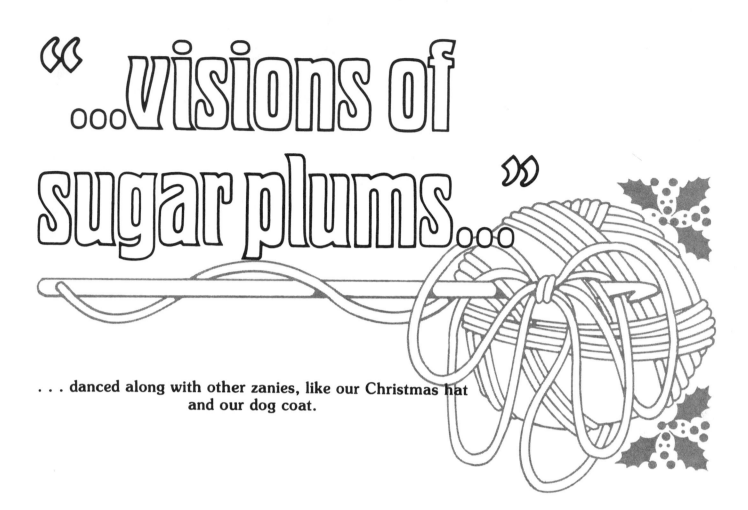

"...visions of sugar plums..."

. . . danced along with other zanies, like our Christmas hat
and our dog coat.

SANTA GIFT TOTE

designed by Carol Wilson Mansfield

Our Santa tote is not only a festive decoration, but
also a practical container for gifts of homemade
goodies—cookies, candies, fruitcakes. You can
even bake the fruitcake right in the coffee can!

Size

Fits over 2-lb coffee can

Materials

Worsted weight yarn:
    2½ oz red
    2½ oz white
    ¼ oz pink
    2 yds blue
Aluminum crochet hook size H (or size required for
    gauge)
2-lb coffee can
Tapestry needle for embroidery

Gauge

In hdc, 10 sts = 3″; 3 rnds = 1″

Pattern Stitch

LOOP STITCH (abbreviated LS): Insert hook into stitch; YO, draw up lp in st (3 lps now on hook);
wrap yarn twice around tip of left index finger; insert
hook in front of yarn and through first lp on finger
(**Fig 1**), draw lp through one lp on hook; bring left
index finger down in front of work; sk first lp on
finger and insert hook through 2nd lp on finger (**Fig
2**), draw lp through 3 lps on hook; drop long lp off
finger = LS made.

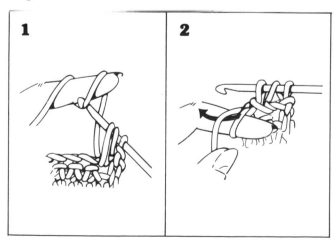

Instructions

Beg at bottom, with red ch 4, join with a sl st to form a ring. [*NOTE: All rnds are worked on right side.*]

Rnd 1: Ch 2 (counts as first hdc of rnd), work 9 hdc in ring, join with a sl st in top of beg ch-2. *(NOTE: Join all following rnds in same manner unless otherwise specified.)*

Rnd 2: Ch 2, hdc in same ch as joining; 2 hdc in each of next 9 hdc, join = 20 hdc.

Rnd 3: Ch 2, 2 hdc in next hdc; * hdc in next hdc, 2 hdc in next hdc; rep from * around, join = 30 hdc.

Rnd 4: Ch 2, hdc in next hdc, 2 hdc in next hdc; * hdc in each of next 2 hdc, 2 hdc in next hdc; rep from * around, join = 40 hdc.

Rnd 5: Ch 2, hdc in each of next 2 hdc, 2 hdc in next hdc; * hdc in each of next 3 hdc, 2 hdc in next hdc; rep from * around, join = 50 hdc.

Rnd 6: Ch 2, hdc in each of next 3 hdc, 2 hdc in next hdc; * hdc in each of next 4 hdc, 2 hdc in next hdc; rep from * around, join = 60 hdc.

Rnd 7: Ch 2, hdc in **back lp only** (lp away from you) in each of rem 59 hdc, join.

Rnd 8: Rep Rnd 7.

Continue by working in **both lps** of sts.

Rnd 9: Ch 2, hdc in each of rem 59 hdc around, join.

Rnds 10 and 11: Rep Rnd 9, twice.

Rnd 12: Ch 2, hdc in each of next 24 hdc; hdc in next st changing to white [**To change colors: Work hdc until 3 lps rem on hook; drop color just used, hook new color and draw through 3 lps on hook = color changed**]. Carry red by placing on top of row and work following sts over it. Work LS in next st and in each of next 7 sts, hdc in next st changing to red as before; finish off white. With red, hdc in each of rem 25 hdc, join.

Rnd 13: Ch 2, hdc in each of next 22 sts, hdc in next st changing to white. Carrying red as before and continuing with white, LS in each of next 13 sts, hdc in next st changing to red; finish off white. With red, hdc in each of rem 22 hdc, join.

Rnd 14: Ch 2, hdc in each of next 21 sts, hdc in next st changing to white. Carrying red and continuing with white, LS in each of next 16 sts, hdc in next st changing to red; finish off white. With red, hdc in each of rem 20 hdc, join changing to white [**To change colors: Insert hook in st, drop color just used; hook new color and draw through = color changed**]. Finish off red.

Rnd 15: Ch 2, LS in same st as joining and in each rem st around, join with a sl st in beg LS = 60 LS.

Rnds 16 and 17: Rep Rnd 15, twice.

Rnd 18: Ch 2, LS in same st as joining; LS in each of next 25 sts, hdc in next st changing to pink. Carrying white and continuing with pink, hdc in **back lp only** in each of next 12 sts, hdc **in back lp only** of next st changing to white; finish off pink. Continue by working in both lps of sts. With white, LS in each of rem 20 sts, join with a sl st in beg LS.

Rnd 19: Ch 2, LS in same st as joining; LS in each of next 25 sts, hdc in next st changing to pink; finish off white. With pink, hdc in each of next 13 sts, hdc in next st changing to white; finish off pink. With white, LS in each of rem 19 sts, join with a sl st in beg LS.

Rnd 20: Ch 2, LS in same st as joining; LS in each of next 25 sts, hdc in next st changing to pink; finish off white. With pink, hdc in each of next 14 sts, hdc in next st changing to white; finish off pink. With white, LS in each of rem 18 sts, join with a sl st in beg LS.

Rnd 21: Ch 2, LS in same st as joining; LS in each of next 25 sts, hdc in next st changing to pink; finish off white. With pink, hdc in each of next 15 sts, hdc in next st changing to white; finish off pink. With white, LS, in each of rem 17 sts, join with a sl st in beg LS.

Rnd 22: Ch 1, sc in same st as joining and in each st around, join with a sl st in beg sc = 60 sc.

Rnds 23 through 25: Rep Rnd 22, 3 times.

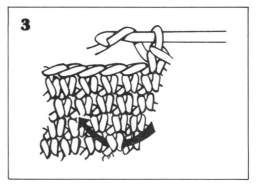

Rnd 26: Ch 1, sc in same sc as joining; work popcorn (abbreviated PC) around post of 2nd sc in 4th rnd below (*Fig 3*) [**To make PC: Work 5 dc from front to back to front around post of sc, remove hook and insert in first dc of 5-dc group; hook dropped lp and pull through (*Fig 4*), ch 1 = PC made**]. * Return to working rnd, sc in next sc (behind PC) and in each of next 2 sc. Return to 4th rnd below, sk 2 sc from last PC, work PC around post of next sc; rep from * around to last 2 sc in working rnd, sc in each of last 2 sc, join with a sl st in beg sc changing to red. Finish off white.

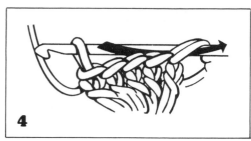

4

Rnd 27: Ch 3, dc in each of next 59 sts (do not work in PCs), join with a sl st in top of beg ch-3.

Rnds 28 through 35: Rep Rnd 27, 8 times. Finish off, weave in all ends.

Finishing

Drawstrings: With red, make two chains each to measure approx 24″ long. Beg and ending at same side of hat, weave one chain through every 2 dcs of last rnd. Then weave other chain in same manner, beg and ending at opposite side of hat and weaving through same sts. Make two white 2″ diameter pompons (see Pompon instructions on page 11). Attach one pompon securely to both ends of each chain.

Facial features: Referring to photo for position, embroider features as follows. For nose, use pink doubled and go over 3 rows (top white row of beard and first 2 pink rows of face) about 8 times, keeping yarn loose to form a "puffy" nose. For each eye, use blue doubled and go over 2nd and 3rd rows of face about 4 times.

DOG CHRISTMAS COAT

designed by Mary Thomas for Nicholas

No reason for the family dog (no matter what his size) to go unadorned for Christmas! Here's a coat designed especially for the family pet to wear at holiday time.

Sizes

	Small	Medium	Large
approx length	10″	14″	20″

NOTE: Length is measured from base of neck to base of tail. Instructions are written for sizes as follows: Small (Medium-Large).

Materials

Worsted weight yarn:
    3(4-8) oz red
    ½(½-1) oz black
    ¼(½-1) oz white
Aluminum crochet hook size G (or size required for gauge)
¾″ metal buckle
⅝″ diameter metal button.

Gauge

In sc, 4 sts = 1″; 4 rows = 1″

Instructions

With red, ch 19(25-43). [*NOTE: Throughout patt, ch 1 and turn to beg each row unless otherwise specified.*]

Row 1: Sc in 2nd ch from hook and in each rem ch across = 18(24-42) sc.

Row 2: Work 2 sc in first sc (inc made), sc in each sc to last sc, inc in last sc = 20(26-44) sc.

Rep Row 2, 3(5-7) times more = 26(36-58) sc. Then inc one sc at beg and end EOR 6(7-9) times = 38(50-76) sc. Work even in sc for 4½ (7-10½)″. Then inc one sc at beg and end EOR 2(3-5) times = 42(56-86) sc.

SHOULDER SHAPING: First Half: Row 1: Inc in first sc, sc in each of next 12(17-26) sc. [Center 16(20-32) sc are left unworked for neck opening; rem 13(18-27) sc will be worked later for other shoulder.]

Row 2: Work a sc dec over first 2 sc, sc in each rem sc across = 13(18-27) sc.

Row 3: Sc in each sc to last 2 sc, dec = 12(17-26) sc.

Rep Rows 2 and 3, 0 (1-2) times more = 12 (15-22) sc, then rep Row 2 once = 11 (14-21) sc. Now dec one sc at beg and end EOR 2(2-4) times = 7(10-13) sc.

Buttonhole Row: Dec, sc in each of next 1(2-4) sc, ch 2, sk 2 sc, sc in each of next 0(2-3) sc, dec over last 2 sc.

Next Row: Sc in each sc and ch-2 sp across. Finish off.

Second Half: Hold piece with shoulder just worked at upper right-hand corner. Sk center 16(20-32) sc and join red yarn with a sl st in next sc.

Row 1: Ch 1, sc in same sc as joining and in each sc to last sc, inc = 14(19-28) sc.

Row 2: Sc in each sc to last 2 sc, dec = 13(18-27) sc.

Row 3: Dec over first 2 sc, sc in each rem sc across = 12(17-26) sc.

Rep Rows 2 and 3, 0(1-2) times more = 12(15-22) sc; then rep Row 2 once = 11(14-21) sc. Now dec one sc at beg and end EOR 2(2-4) times = 7(10-13) sc.

Buttonhole Row: Dec, sc in each of next 0(2-3) sc, ch 2, sk 2 sc, sc in each of next 1(2-4) sc, dec over last 2 sc.

Next Row: Sc in each sc and ch-2 sp across. Finish off, weave in yarn ends.

FRONT: With red, ch 5(7-9).

Row 1: Sc in 2nd ch from hook and in each rem ch across = 4(6-8) sc.

Row 2: Sc in each sc across.

Row 3: Inc in first sc, sc in each sc to last sc, inc in last sc = 6(8-10) sc.

Rep Rows 2 and 3, 6(9-14) times more = 18(26-38) sc.

Work even in sc for 1½(2-2½)″. Finish off.

BELT: Row 1: With black, ch 24(28-32), sc in each of 18 (26-38) sc across last row worked of Front, then ch 25(29-33).

Row 2: Sc in 2nd ch from hook and in each of rem 23(27-31) chs; sc in each of 18(26-38) sc across Front, sc in each of rem 24(28-32) ch = 66 (82-102) sc.

Rows 3 and 4: Sc in each sc across. Finish off, weave in all yarn ends.

Finishing

Sew buckle to one end of belt. Sew button to front approx 3 rows from beg edge; button front to back at shoulders. With white, make 2(3-4) 2″ diameter pompons (see page 11) and attach them evenly spaced at center neck edge of back.

BABY'S SANTA HAT

designed by Barbara Retzke

When the new baby arrives at Grandma's house on Christmas morning with his replica of Santa's hat designed especially for infants, even Scrooge will say, "Merry Christmas!"

Size

6 to 12 months

Materials

Worsted weight yarn:
    1½ oz red
Mohair-type yarn:
    1 oz white
Aluminum crochet hook size G (or size required for gauge)
One jingle bell

Gauge

With worsted weight yarn in hdc, 7 sts = 2″; 5 rnds = 2″

Instructions

Beg at ribbed cuff with white, ch 17.

Row 1: Sc in 2nd ch from hook and in each rem ch across = 16 sc.

Row 2: Ch 1, turn; sc **in back lp only** of each sc across. Rep Row 2 for a total of 60 rows. Fold cuff in half and sl st across last row completed and first row, carefully matching sts; finish off. Join red with a sl st in end st of last row worked. [*NOTE: You will now work in rnds; beg ch of each rnd counts as one st.*]

Rnd 1: Ch 2, hdc in next row and in each row of ribbed cuff, join with a sl st in top of beg ch-2 = 60 sts.

Rnd 2: Ch 2, hdc in next st and in each st around. (*NOTE: At end of this rnd and all following rnds, join with a sl st in top of beg ch.*)

Rnd 3: Ch 2, hdc in each of next 4 sts, work a hdc dec over next 2 sts; * hdc in each of next 10 sts, work a hdc dec; rep from * 3 times, hdc in each of last 5 sts = 55 sts.

Rnd 4: Rep Rnd 2.

Rnd 5: Ch 2, hdc in each of next 4 sts, dec; * hdc in each of next 9 sts, dec; rep from * 3 times, hdc in each of last 4 sts = 50 sts.

Rnd 6: Rep Rnd 2.

Rnd 7: Ch 2, hdc in each of next 3 sts, dec; * hdc in each of next 8 sts, dec; rep from * 3 times, hdc in each of last 4 sts = 45 sts.

Rnd 8: Ch 3, dc in next st and in each st around.

Rnd 9: Ch 3, dc in next st, work a dc dec over next 2 sts; * dc in each of next 3 dc, work a dc dec; rep from * 7 times, dc in last st = 36 sts.

Rnd 10: Rep Rnd 8.

Rnd 11: Ch 3, dc in next st, dec; * dc in each of next 2 sts, dec; rep from * 7 times = 27 sts.

Rnd 12: Rep Rnd 8.

Rnd 13: Ch 3, * dc in next st, dec; rep from * 7 times, dc in each of last 2 sts = 19 sts.

Rnd 14: Rep Rnd 8.

Rnd 15: Ch 3, dec nine times = 10 sts.

Rnd 16: Rep Rnd 8. Finish off, leaving approx 12″ length; thread into tapestry needle. Weave yarn end through rem sts and draw up tightly and fasten securely on inside.

Finishing

With white, make 2″ diameter pompon (see page 11); attach jingle bell at center and sew securely to tip of hat.

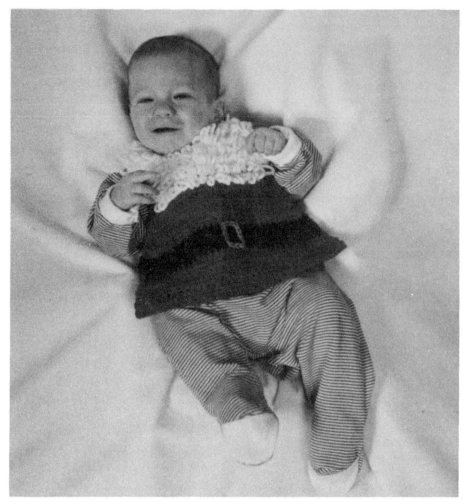

BABY'S SANTA BIB

designed by Mary Thomas

Let the smallest member of the family join in the holiday fun with his bib designed to look like Santa's suit.

Materials

Worsted weight yarn:
    1 oz red
    ½ oz white
    ¼ oz black
    24" strand gold
Aluminum crochet hook Size G (or size required for
  gauge)
⅝" diameter white button

GAUGE

In hdc, 7 sts = 2"

Pattern Stitch

FRONT LOOP STITCH (*abbreviated flp*): With right side of work facing, insert hook into st; hook yarn and draw a lp through st (2 lps now on hook). Wrap yarn twice around tip of left index finger, insert hook in front of yarn and through first lp on finger (**Fig 1**), draw lp through one lp on hook. Bring left index finger down in front of work, skip first

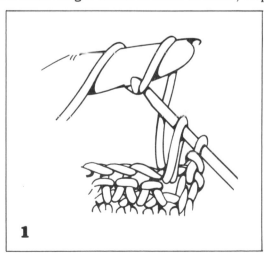

1

117

lp on finger and insert hook through 2nd lp on finger (*Fig 2*), draw lp through both rem lps on hook. Drop long lp off finger. One flp made.

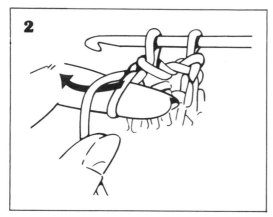

Instructions

With red, ch 36 loosely. (*NOTE: Ch 2 counts as one hdc.*)

Row 1 (Wrong Side): Hdc in 3rd ch from hook and in each rem ch across = 35 hdc.

Row 2: Ch 2, turn; hdc in next hdc and in each hdc across, ending hdc in top of Tch.

Rows 3 through 6: Rep Row 2 four times. At end of last row, change to black as follows. Work hdc in top of Tch until there are 3 lps on hook; finish off red, hook black yarn leaving 4″ end and draw through all lps on hook.

Rows 7 through 9: With black, rep Row 2 three times. At end of last row change to red.

Row 10: Rep Row 2.

Row 11: Ch 2, turn; work a hdc dec over next 2 hdc, hdc in each hdc to last 3 hdc; work a hdc dec, hdc in top of Tch = 33 hdc.

Rows 12 through 15: Rep Rows 10 and 11 twice; at end of Row 15, you should have 29 hdc.

Row 16: Ch 2, turn; dec over next 2 hdc, hdc in next hdc, hdc in next hdc changing to white. **Do not finish off red**; instead lay red on top of row and work each st over it. Work a flp in each of next 18 hdc, flp in next hdc changing to red as follows. Work st until left index finger is brought down in front of work; drop white, hook red yarn and draw through both lps on hook. Hdc in each of next 2 hdc, dec over next 2 hdc, hdc in top of Tch = 27 sts.

Row 17: Ch 1, turn; sc in each of first 2 hdc, sc in next hdc changing to white as follows: Insert hook in st and draw up a lp; drop red, hook white and draw through both lps now on hook. Working over red as before, sc in each of next 20 sts, sc in next st changing to red; sc in each of next 2 hdc, sc in top of Tch = 27 sc.

Row 18: Ch 1, turn; sc in first sc, sc in next sc changing to white. Working over red, flp in each sc to last 3 sc, sc in next sc changing to red; sc in each of last 2 sc. Finish off red; continue with white only.

Row 19: Ch 1, turn; sc in each st across = 27 sc.

Row 20: Ch 1, turn; flp in each sc to last sc, sc in last sc.

Rows 21 through 26: Rep Rows 19 and 20 three times. Do not finish off; continue with neck shaping.

Right Neck Shaping: Row 1: Ch 1, turn; work a sc dec over first 2 sts, sc in each of next 6 sts = 7 sc [center 11 sts are left unworked for neck opening; rem 8 sts will be worked later for left neck shaping].

Row 2: Ch 1, turn; flp in each sc to last sc, sc in last sc.

Row 3: Ch 1, turn; dec, sc in each rem sc across = 6 sc.

Rows 4 and 5: Rep Rows 2 and 3 = 5 sc.

Row 6: Rep Row 2.

Row 7: Ch 1, turn; sc in each sc across.

Rows 8 and 9: Rep Rows 2 and 7.

Rows 10 through 13: Rep Rows 4 through 7.

Rows 14 and 15: Rep Rows 2 and 3 = 3 sc.

Row 16: Rep Row 7. Finish off.

Left Neck Shaping: With wrong side facing and shaping just worked to your right, sk center 11 sts and join white with a sl st in next st, ch 1.

Row 1: Sc in same st as joining and in each of next 5 sts, dec over last 2 sts = 7 sc.

Row 2: Ch 1, turn; flp in each sc to last sc, sc in last sc.

Row 3: Ch 1, turn; sc in each st to last 2 sts, dec = 6 sc.

Rows 4 and 5: Rep Rows 2 and 3 = 5 sc.

Row 6: Rep Row 2.

Row 7: Ch 1, turn; sc in each sc across.

Rows 8 and 9: Rep Rows 2 and 7.

Rows 10 through 13: Rep Rows 4 through 7.

Rows 14 and 15: Rep Rows 2 and 3 = 3 sc.

Row 16 (Buttonhole Row): Ch 1, turn; sc in first sc, ch 2, sk one sc, sc in last sc. Finish off, weave in all yarn ends.

Finishing

Sew button to end of right neck shaping. Thread gold yarn into tapestry needle and embroider chain sts for buckle.

TINY TREASURES

designed by Mary Thomas and Kathie Schroeder

A wonderful collection of quick and easy little designs that can be tied on a tree, used to decorate a package, or even worn on your coat lapel.

SANTA

Size
Approx 3″ tall without pompon

Materials
Sport weight yarn:
    5 yds white
    2 yds each pink and red
    12″ strand blue
Aluminum crochet hook size F (or size required for gauge)
Tapestry needle for embroidery

Gauge
In sc, 9 sts = 2″

Instructions
With pink, ch 4, join with a sl st to form a ring.

Rnd 1 (right side): Ch 3, work 4 dc in ring; work next dc in ring changing to white [**To change col-**

119

ors: **Work st until 2 lps rem on hook; drop color being used, hook new color and draw through 2 lps on hook = color changed**]. Carry pink by placing on top of ring and work the following sts over it. With white, work 6 more dc in ring, join with a sl st in top of beg ch-3 changing to pink [**To change colors in joining sl st: Insert hook in st; drop color being used, hook new color and draw through = color changed**].

Rnd 2: Continuing with pink and carrying white, ch 1, do not turn; 2 sc in same ch as joining; 2 sc in each of next 5 dc changing to white in last st; finish off pink and continue with white only; 2 sc in each of rem 6 dc, join with a sl st in beg sc.

Rnd 3 (beard and hat trim): Ch 5, turn; sl st in next sc, * ch 5, sl st in next sc; rep from * 10 times more; ch 1, sk next 2 sc, sc in each of next 8 sc; sk next sc, sl st in next sc; finish off white.

HAT: Turn; with right side facing, join red with sl st in **back lp only** of last sc of prev rnd.

Row 1: Ch 3, working in **back lp only** of each st across, dc in each of next 6 sc, hdc in next sc. Continue by working in **both lps** of sts.

Row 2: Ch 2, turn; hdc in each of next 5 dc, sc in next dc.

Row 3: Ch 1, turn; sk first sc, work sc decrease (dec) over next 2 hdc [**To dec: Draw up a lp in each of 2 sts, YO and draw through all 3 lps on hook = dec made**]. Sc in next hdc, dec over next 2 hdc as before.

Row 4: Ch 1, turn; dec over first 2 sc, sl st in next sc. Finish off, weave in all ends.

Finishing

Make ½" diameter white pompon (see Pompon instructions on page 11) and attach to top of hat. Use single strand of blue and embroider one cross stitch for each eye as shown in photo.

POINSETTIA

Size
Approx 6" diameter

Materials

Sport weight yarn:
18 yds red
5 yds bright yellow
Aluminum crochet hook size G (or size required for gauge)

Gauge

In sc, 4 sts = 1"

Instructions

With yellow, ch 2.

Rnd 1 (right side): Work 6 sc in 2nd ch from hook, join with a sl st in beg sc.

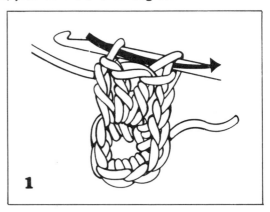

Rnd 2: Work beg PC (popcorn) in same sc as joining [**To make beg PC: Ch 3, work 3 dc in st; remove hook and insert in top of ch-3; hook dropped lp and pull through (*Fig 1*) = beg PC made**] * Ch 2, work PC in next sc [**To make PC: Work 4 dc in st; remove hook and insert in first dc of 4-dc group; hook dropped lp and pull through = PC made**]; rep from * 4 times more, ch 2, join with a sl st in top of ch-3 of beg PC = 6 PC. Finish off yellow.

Rnd 3: With right side facing, join red with a sl st in any ch-2 sp. * Work leaf attaching to same ch-2 sp as follows:

Row 1: With right side facing, ch 4, sc in 2nd ch from hook and in each of rem 2 chs; sl st back into same ch-2 sp.

Row 2: Ch 1, turn; with wrong side facing, sc in each sc across = 3 sc.

Row 3: Ch 4, turn; with right side facing, sc in 2nd ch from hook and in each of next 2 chs; sc in each of next 3 sc, sl st back into same ch-2 sp.

Row 4: Rep Row 2 = 6 sc.

Row 5: Ch 4, turn; with right side facing, sc in 2nd ch from hook and in each of next 2 chs; † ch 2, sl st in first ch of ch-2 just made †; sc in next sc, hdc in each of next 2 sc; rep from † to † once; dc in each of next 2 sc; rep from † to † once; (dc, hdc) in last sc, sl st back into same ch-2 sp. [One leaf is now completed.] Working behind PC, sl st into next ch-2 sp; rep from * 5 times more, ending last rep by working sl st into beg ch-2 sp (where first leaf was worked). Finish off, weave in all ends.

HOLLY

WREATH

Size

Approx 3½″ diameter

Materials

Sport weight yarn:
    15 yds green
    40″ strand red
Aluminum crochet hook size F (or size required for gauge)

Gauge

In cluster st, 3 sts = 1″

Instructions

With green, ch 24, join with sl st in **top lp only** of first ch to form a ring, being careful not to twist chain.

Rnd 1: Ch 1, sc in same st as joining; sc in **top lp only** in each of next 23 chs, join with a sl st in beg sc.

Rnd 2: Pull up lp on hook to measure ½″; work cluster st in same st as joining [**To make cluster st: † YO, insert hook in st and draw up ½″ lp; YO and draw through 2 lps on hook †; rep from † to † twice; YO and draw through all 4 lps on hook, ch 1 = cluster st made**]; work cluster st in each rem sc around, join with a sl st in ch-1 at top of beg cluster st.

Rnd 3: Ch 1, sc in same st as joining; * sc in sp at top of next cluster st (where yarn was drawn through 4 lps of st), sc in ch-1 of same cluster st; rep from * around, join with a sl st in beg sc. Finish off, weave in yarn ends. Beg at joining and weave red strand doubled through sts in Rnd 1 (where cluster sts were worked); then tie into a bow and trim ends evenly.

Size

Leaf measures approx 2½″ long; diameter of berry measures approx ⅝″.

Materials

American Thread Dawn Sayelle Knitting Worsted Size Yarn:
    ¼ oz each of Golf Green and Flame
Size G aluminum crochet hook (or size required for gauge)

NOTE: Approx 3 yds of Golf Green will make one leaf; approx 1½ yds of Flame will make one berry.

Gauge

In sc, 4 sts = 1″

Instructions

LEAVES (*make 3*): With Golf Green, ch 11. **Working in top lp of each ch,** sl st in 2nd ch from hook, sc in next ch; hdc in next ch, dc in next ch. Work picot as follows: Ch 3, sl st in 3rd ch from hook (*picot made*). Sc in next ch, hdc in next ch; dc in next ch, picot, sc in next ch; sl st in next ch, 3 sl sts in last ch. **Continuing to work on opposite side of starting chain,** sl st in next st, sc in next st; dc in next st, picot, sc in next st, hdc in next st; dc in next st, picot, sc in next st, sl st in each of last 3 sts. Finish off: weave in ends (or if sewing length is needed, leave approx 6″ end).

BERRIES (*make 3*): With Flame, ch 2.

Rnd 1: Work 6 sc in 2nd ch from hook, do not join; work continuous rnds.

Rnd 2: Sc in each sc around.

Rnd 3: Rep Rnd 2. Finish off, leaving approx 6″ sewing length. Thread into tapestry or yarn needle and weave through sts of last rnd. Draw up tightly and fasten securely.

Tie leaves and berries onto package, using strand of Flame or Golf Green yarn.

"...the sleigh full of toys..."

. . . especially created for that favorite child because Christmas just wouldn't be Christmas without "a bundle of toys. . . ."

BIG BEAR

designed by Louise O'Donnell

Make a giant, huggable bear for your favorite child. He sports his own warm scarf and perky hat. Made in durable rug yarn, this toy works up very quicky.

Size
Approx 24″ tall (in sitting position)

Materials
Aunt Lydia's Heavy Rug Yarn in 70-yd skeins:
    16 skeins Brown
    1 skein Wood Brown
    2 skeins each of Red and National Blue
Size G aluminum crochet hook (or size required for gauge)
6 lbs Polyester fiber (for stuffing)

Gauge
In hdc, 7 sts = 2″

NOTE: It is absolutely essential that you work to the exact gauge specified (7 hdc = 2″) to obtain the shape of the toy as shown in photo.

Instructions
BODY: Beg at bottom, with Brown, ch 2.

Rnd 1: Work 9 sc in 2nd ch from hook. Do not join rnds. Use a small safety pin or piece of yarn in contrasting color and mark first st of rnd; move marker at beg of each rnd.

Rnd 2: Work 2 hdc in each st around = 18 hdc.

Rnd 3: Rep Rnd 2 = 36 hdc.

Rnd 4: * Hdc in each of next 2 sts, 2 hdc in next st; rep from * around = 48 hdc.

Rnd 5: * Work 2 hdc in next st, hdc in each of next 3 sts; rep from * around = 60 hdc.

Rnd 6: * Hdc in each of next 5 sts, 2 hdc in next st; rep from * around = 70 hdc.

Rnd 7 * Hdc in each of next 4 sts, 2 hdc in next st; rep from * around = 84 hdc.

Rnd 8: * Hdc **in back lp** (*lp away from you*) in each of next 2 sts, 2 hdc **in back lp** of next st; rep from * around = 112 hdc.

Rnds 9 through 30: (*NOTE: Continue by working **in both lps** of sts.*) Work 22 rnds even in hdc on 112 sts.

Rnd 31: (*NOTE: Mark first st of rnd for center back;*

use marker different from beg of rnd. Do not move marker.) Hdc in each of next 18 sts. * Work a dec (decrease) as follows: YO (yarn over) hook, insert hook in next st and draw up a lp (3 lps now on hook); insert hook in next st and draw up a lp (4 lps now on hook); YO and draw through all 4 lps on hook (dec made); hdc in each of next 2 sts; rep from * to last 18 sts, hdc in each of rem 18 sts = 93 hdc.

Rnds 32 through 38: Work 7 rnds even in hdc on 93 sts.

Rnds 39: Hdc in each of next 3 hdc; * dec, hdc in each of next 13 hdc; rep from * around = 87 hdc.

Rnds 40 through 43: Work 4 rnds even in hdc on 87 sts.

Rnd 44: Hdc in each of next 3 hdc; * dec, hdc in each of next 19 hdc; rep from * around = 83 hdc.

Rnd 45: Work even in hdc on 83 sts.

Rnd 46: Hdc in each of next 3 hdc; * dec, hdc in each of next 14 hdc; rep from * around = 78 hdc.

Rnds 47 through 49: Work 3 rnds even in hdc on 78 sts.

Stuff body very full and smooth into desired shape with your hands on outside. Then work neck and head as follows.

NECK AND HEAD: Rnd 1: * Hdc in each of next 4 sts, dec; rep from * around = 65 hdc.

Rnd 2: * Hdc in each of next 3 sts, dec; rep from * around = 52 hdc.

Rnd 3: Work even in hdc on 52 sts.

Rnd 4: * Hdc in each of next 3 sts, 2 hdc in next st; rep from * around = 65 hdc.

Rnd 5: * Hdc in each of next 4 sts, 2 hdc in next st; rep from * around = 78 sts.

NOTE: Now you will begin shaping cheeks. To be sure back of head is placed directly over center back, you must begin this rnd directly above marker at center back. If necessary, adjust position for beg of next rnd by working in hdc to st above center back marker. Mark this st for beg of rnd; then proceed as follows.

Rnd 6: Hdc in each of next 12 sts, 2 hdc in next st; work (hdc in each of next 2 sts, 2 hdc in next st) 7 times; hdc in each of next 12 sts, work (2 hdc in next st, hdc in each of next 2 sts) 7 times; hdc in each of rem 11 sts = 93 hdc.

Rnd 7: Hdc in each of next 43 sts, dec; hdc in each of next 3 sts, dec; hdc in each of rem 43 sts = 91 hdc.

Rnds 8 through 13: Work 6 rnds even in hdc on 91 sts.

Rnd 14: (*NOTE: Again be sure this rnd begins directly above marker at center back. If necessary, adjust position as before.*) Hdc in each of next 12 sts, dec; hdc in each of next 22 sts, dec; hdc in each of next 16 sts, dec; hdc in each of next 22 sts, dec; hdc in each of last 11 sts = 87 hdc.

Rnd 15: Hdc in each of next 11 sts, dec; work (hdc in each of next 6 sts, dec) twice; hdc in each of next 5 sts, dec; hdc in each of next 15 sts, dec; hdc in each of next 5 sts, dec; work (hdc in each of next 6 sts, dec) twice; hdc in each of last 11 sts = 79 hdc.

Stuff head firmly, filling out cheeks roundly on each side. From now on, stuff every few rnds.

Rnd 16: Hdc in each of next 12 sts, dec; work (hdc in each of next 6 sts, dec) twice; hdc in each of next 21 sts, work (dec, hdc in each of next 6 sts) twice; dec, hdc in each of last 10 sts = 73 hdc.

Rnd 17: Hdc in each of next 10 sts, work (dec, hdc in next st) 6 times; hdc in each of next 19 sts, work (dec, hdc in next st) 6 times; hdc in each of last 8 sts = 61 hdc.

Rnd 18: Work even in hdc on 61 sts.

Rnd 19: Hdc in next st, * dec, hdc in each of next 8 sts; rep from * around = 55 hdc.

Rnd 20: Hdc in each of next 3 sts, * dec, hdc in each of next 11 sts; rep from * around = 51 hdc.

Rnd 21: * Hdc in each of next 10 sts, dec; rep from * to last 3 sts, hdc in each of last 3 sts = 47 hdc.

Rnd 22: Hdc in each of next 3 sts, * dec, hdc in each of next 9 sts; rep from * around = 43 hdc.

Rnd 23: * Hdc in each of next 8 sts, dec; rep from * to last 3 sts, hdc in each of last 3 sts = 39 hdc.

Rnd 24: * Hdc in each of next 4 sts, dec; rep from * to last 3 sts, hdc in each of last 3 sts = 33 hdc.

Rnd 25: Hdc in next st, (dec) 16 times = 17 hdc.

Rnd 26: Hdc in next st, (dec) 8 times = 9 hdc.

Rnd 27: Sc in next st, * work sc dec as follows. Draw up a lp in each of next 2 sts, YO and draw through all 3 lps on hook (sc dec made). Rep from * around = 5 sc. Finish off, leaving approx 6″ end. Add any extra stuffing, if necessary; sew opening closed tightly.

LEGS (*make 2*): Beg at center of sole, with Brown, ch 4.

Rnd 1: Work 3 sc in 2nd ch from hook, 2 sc in next ch, 3 sc in last ch. Continuing on opposite side of chain, work 2 sc in next ch = 10 sc. (*Do not join; work continuous rnds. Mark first st of rnd; move marker at beg of each rnd.*)

Rnd 2: * Work 2 sc in each of next 3 sc, sc in each of next 2 sc; rep from * once more = 16 sc.

Rnd 3: * Work 2 hdc in each of next 6 sc, hdc in each of next 2 sc; rep from * once more = 28 hdc.

Rnd 4: Hdc in each of next 2 sts, 2 hdc in each of next 8 sts; hdc in each of next 6 sts, 2 hdc in each of next 8 sts; hdc in each of last 4 sts = 44 hdc.

Rnd 5: Hdc in each of next 7 sts, 2 hdc in each of next 8 sts; hdc in each of next 14 sts, 2 hdc in each of next 8 sts; hdc in each of last 7 sts = 60 hdc.

Rnd 6: Hdc in each of next 10 sts, work (2 hdc in next st, hdc in next st) 6 times; hdc in each of next 19 sts, work (2 hdc in next st, hdc in next st) 4 times; hdc in each of next 10 sts, sc in last st = 70 sts.

Rnd 7: Hdc **in back lp** of each st around. Sole is now completed; continue by working foot and leg as follows.

Rnd 8: (*NOTE: Continue to work* **in both lps** *of sts.*) Hdc in each of next 9 sts, work (dec, hdc in next st) 7 times; hdc in each rem st around = 63 hdc.

Rnd 9: Hdc in each of next 7 sts, work (dec, hdc in next st) 6 times; hdc in each rem st around = 57 hdc.

Rnds 10 through 13: Work 4 rnds even in hdc on 57 sts.

Rnd 14: Hdc in each of next 12 sts, dec; hdc in each of next 6 sts, dec; hdc in each rem st around = 55 hdc.

Rnds 15 and 16: Work 2 rnds even in hdc on 55 sts.

Rnd 17: Hdc in each of next 14 sts, dec; hdc in each of next 2 sts, dec; hdc in each rem st around = 53 hdc.

Rnds 18 and 19: Work 2 rnds even in hdc on 53 sts.

Rnd 20: Hdc in next st, * dec, hdc in each of next 11 sts; rep from * around = 49 hdc.

Rnds 21 through 23: Work 3 rnds even in hdc on 49 sts.

Rnd 24: Hdc in next st, * dec, hdc in each of next 10 sts; rep from * around = 45 hdc.

Rnds 25 through 27: Work 3 rnds even in hdc on 45 sts.

Rnd 28: Hdc in next st, * dec, hdc in each of next 9 sts; rep from * around = 41 hdc.

Rnds 29 and 30: Work 2 rnds even in hdc on 41 sts. At end of last rnd, finish off, leaving approx 18″ sewing length.

Stuff leg firmly to last 2 rnds at top; leave 2 top rnds very lightly stuffed so leg will be able to bend when attached to body.

Sew top of leg closed; then sew leg to bottom of body.

ARMS (*make 2*): Beg at bottom of paw, with Brown, ch 2.

Rnd 1: Work 7 sc in 2nd ch from hook. Do not join; mark first st of rnd as before.

Rnd 2: Work 2 sc in each sc around = 14 sc.

Rnd 3: * Hdc in next sc, 2 hdc in next sc; rep from * around = 21 hdc.

Rnd 4: * Work 2 hdc in next st, hdc in each of next 2 sts; rep from * around = 28 hdc.

Rnds 5 and 6: Work 2 rnds even in hdc on 28 sts.

Rnd 7: Hdc in each of next 14 sts, 3 hdc in next st; hdc in each of rem 13 sts = 30 hdc.

Rnd 8: Hdc in next st, 2 hdc in next st; hdc in each of next 12 sts, 2 hdc in each of next 3 sts; hdc in each st around to last st, 2 hdc in last st = 35 hdc.

Rnd 9: Hdc in each of next 15 sts, 2 hdc in each of next 6 sts; hdc in each of rem 14 sts = 41 hdc.

Rnd 10: Work even in hdc on 41 sts.

Rnd 11: Hdc in each of next 18 sts, (dec) 3 times, hdc in each rem st around = 38 hdc.

Rnds 12 through 18: Work 7 rnds even in hdc on 38 sts.

Rnd 19: * Dec, hdc in each of next 17 sts; rep from * once more = 36 hdc.

Rnds 20 and 21: Work 2 rnds even in hdc on 36 sts.

Rnd 22: * Dec, hdc in each of next 16 sts; rep from * once more = 34 hdc.

Rnds 23 and 24: Work 2 rnds even in hdc on 34 sts.

Rnd 25: * Dec, hdc in each of next 15 sts; rep from * once more = 32 hdc.

Rnds 26 through 28: Work 3 rnds even in hdc on 32 sts. At end of last rnd, finish off, leaving approx 24″ sewing length.

Stuff arm firmly to last 2 rnds at top, carefully poking stuffing down into paw. Stuff 2 top rnds very lightly so arm will be able to bend when attached to body.

Sew top of arm closed; then sew arm to side of body at shoulder.

EARS (*make 2*): With Brown, ch 6.

Row 1: Work 2 hdc in 3rd ch from hook and in each of next 3 chs = 8 hdc.

Row 2: Ch 2 (*do not count as one st*), turn; hdc in first st, work (hdc, dc) in next st; 2 dc in each of next 3 sts, work (dc, hdc) in next st; 2 hdc in next st, sc in last st.

Row 3: Ch 1, turn; sc in first st, 2 hdc in next st; work (hdc, dc) in next st, 2 dc in next st; work (dc, tr) in next st [**To work tr: YO hook twice, insert**

hook in st and draw up a lp—4 lps now on hook; work (YO and draw through 2 lps on hook) 3 times = tr made]. Work 2 tr in each of next 5 sts, work (tr, dc) in next st; work 2 dc in next st, work (dc hdc) in next st; sc in last st. Finish off, leaving approx 12″ sewing length.

Sew ear to side of head at top.

SNOUT: With Brown, ch 2.

Rnd 1: Work 7 sc in 2nd ch from hook. Do not join; mark first st of rnd as before.

Rnd 2: Work 2 hdc in each sc around = 14 hdc.

Rnd 3: * Hdc in next st, 2 hdc in next st; rep from * around = 21 hdc.

Rnd 4: Hdc in next st * hdc in next st, 2 hdc in next st; rep from * around = 31 hdc.

Rnds 5 and 6: Work 2 rnds even in hdc on 31 sts.

Rnd 7: Hdc in next st, * hdc in each of next 2 sts, 2 hdc in next st; rep from * around = 41 hdc.

Rnd 8: Work (hdc in each of next 3 sts, 2 hdc in next st) 9 times, hdc in each of rem 5 sts = 50 hdc. Now work sc in next st, sl st in next st; then finish off, leaving approx 18″ sewing length.

Stuff snout firmly and sew to center front of face between cheeks.

NOSE TIP: With Wood Brown, ch 2.

Rnd 1: Work 7 sc in 2nd ch from hook. Do not join.

Rnd 2: Work 2 sc in each sc around = 14 sc. Now work sl st in next st; then finish off, leaving approx 12″ sewing length.

Sew to front of snout, positioned slightly above center.

EYES, TUMMY BUTTON, SMALL PADS (for front paws and feet) (make 19 pieces): With Wood Brown, ch 2. Work 7 sc in 2nd ch from hook, join with a sl st in beg sc. Finish off, leaving approx 12″ sewing length.

For eyes, sew 2 pieces to face just above snout, having 6 sts between eyes.

For tummy button, sew one piece to center front of body, approx 4½″ above crotch.

For paw pads, sew 4 pieces evenly spaced to each upper outer edge of each foot sole and each front paw, as in photo.

LARGE PADS (for front paws and feet) (make 4): With Wood Brown, ch 2.

Rnd 1: Work 7 sc in 2nd ch from hook. (Do not join.)

Rnd 2: Work 2 sc in each sc around = 14 sc.

Rnd 3: * Sc in next sc, 2 sc in next sc; rep from *

around = 21 sc. Join with a sl st in beg sc. Finish off, leaving approx 12″ sewing length.

Sew one piece to each foot sole and front paw below smaller pads.

SCARF: With National Blue, ch 18.

Row 1: Hdc in 3rd ch from hook and in each rem ch across = 16 hdc.

Row 2: Ch 2 (do not count as one st), turn; hdc in each st across, changing to Red in last hdc. (**To change colors: Work hdc until 3 lps rem on hook. Drop color being used; do not cut—color is carried loosely up side of work. With new color YO and draw through all 3 lps on hook = color changed.**)

Row 3: With Red, ch 3 (counts as one dc), turn; dc in next st and in each rem st across = 16 dc (counting ch-3).

Row 4: Ch 3, turn; dc in next st and in each rem st across, changing to National Blue in last dc (remember to work last dc in top of ch-3). (**To change colors: Work dc until 2 lps rem on hook. Drop color being used; with new color, YO and draw through both lps on hook = color changed.**)

Rows 5 and 6: With National Blue, rep Rows 3 and 4. At end of Row 6, change to Red in last dc.

Row 7: With Red, ch 3, turn; work dc dec as follows. * YO and draw up a lp in next st, YO and draw through 2 lps on hook; rep from * once more (*3 lps now on hook*); YO and draw through all 3 lps on hook = dc dec made. Dc in each rem st across = 15 dc.

Row 8: Rep Row 7, changing to National Blue in last dc = 14 dc.

Rows 9 through 20: Rep Rows 5 through 8, three times more. At end of Row 20, you should have 8 dc.

Continuing to alternate colors every 2 rows, work even in dc on 8 sts until 15 stripes of National Blue have been completed (*count from beg edge*). Continue with Red and work increase shaping as follows.

Row 1: With Red, ch 3, turn; work 2 dc in next st (*increase made*), dc in each rem st across = 9 dc.

Row 2: Rep Row 1, changing to National Blue in last dc = 10 dc.

Row 3: With National Blue, ch 3, turn; dc in next st and in each rem st across.

Row 4: Rep Row 3, changing to Red in last dc.

Rows 5 through 16: Rep prev Rows 1 through 4, three times. At end of Row 16, you should have 16 dc.

Rows 17 and 18: With Red, rep prev Row 3, twice. At end of Row 18, change to National Blue in last dc. Finish off Red.

Row 19: Continuing with National Blue only, ch 2, turn; hdc in first st and in each rem st across, ending by working hdc in top of ch-3 = 16 hdc (*remember ch-2 does not count as one st*).

Row 20: Ch 2, turn; hdc in each st across. Do not finish off. Ch 1, work an edging in sc evenly spaced (*approx 2 sts in each row and one st in each st across each end, with 3 sts in each corner*) around all 4 sides of scarf. Join with a sl st in beg sc. Finish off; weave in all ends. Place scarf around neck and tie at center front.

HAT: Beg at top, with National Blue, ch 2.

Rnd 1: Work 9 sc in 2nd ch from hook. Do not join.

Rnd 2: Work 2 sc in each sc around, changing to Red in last sc. **(To change colors: Work sc until 2 lps rem on hook. Drop color being used; do not cut — carry color not in use across back of work. With new color, YO and draw through 2 lps on hook = color changed.)** You should now have 18 sc. Join with a sl st in beg sc.

Rnd 3: With Red, ch 3, 2 dc in next st; * dc in next st, 2 dc in next st; rep from * around, changing to National Blue in last dc. You should now have 27 dc (*counting ch-3*). Join with a sl st in top of beg ch-3.

Rnd 4: With National Blue, ch 3, dc in next st and in each rem st around; join with a sl st in top of beg ch-3.

Rnds 5 through 7: Rep Rnd 4, three times. At end of Rnd 7, change to Red in last dc, then join with a sl st in top of beg ch-3.

Rnd 8: With Red, Rep Rnd 4, changing to National Blue in last dc; then join with a sl st in top of beg ch-3. Finish off Red.

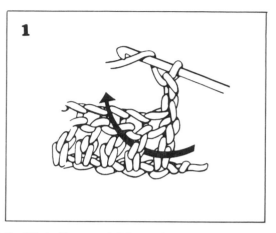

Rnd 9: With National Blue, ch 3, turn; * work dc around post (from front to back to front) of next st (*Fig 1*), dc in next st; rep from * around. Join with a sl st in top of beg ch-3.

Rnd 10: Ch 3, *do not turn;* * work dc around post of next st, dc in next st; rep from * around. Join with a sl st in top of beg ch-3. Finish off; weave in ends.

Turn last 2 rnds up for cuff. Place hat on head as shown in photo and sew in place.

SISTER SUE AND HER BASKET, TOO

designed by Sue Penrod

This enchanting "take along" crocheted baby comes with a complete wardrobe and lives in her own basket, which doubles as a little girl's purse. Included are panties, bib, booties, bonnet, baby bag and a blanket. The basket has plastic ring handles. It's easy to make and will delight any little girl.

Size

Basket measures approx 8″ wide x 5″ deep (from bottom edge to handles); doll measures approx 6″ tall.

Materials

Worsted weight yarn (*for basket and doll*):
    4 oz white
    1½ oz light pink
    1 oz medium pink
Sport weight yarn (*for doll's hair and layette*):
    1 oz white
    ¼ oz light brown
    ½ oz each of light blue, light pink and
      bright yellow
Sizes D, G and J aluminum crochet hooks (or sizes required for gauge)
2 Brown plastic macrame rings (5″ diameter)—for handles
Polyester fiber (*for stuffing doll and pillow inside basket*)
Small pieces of felt in blue and pink
Tracing paper and pencil
White craft glue
Size 16 tapestry needle or yarn needle

Gauge

With size J hook and worsted weight yarn, 3 dc = 1″
With size G hook and worsted weight yarn, 4 sc = 1″
With size D hook and sport weight yarn, 5 dc = 1″

BASKET

Instructions

LINING: Beg at bottom, with white worsted weight yarn and size J hook (*or size required to obtain gauge of 3 sc per inch*) ch 4. Join with a sl st to form a ring.

Rnd 1: Work 2 sc in each ch around = 8 sc. Do not join; work continuous rnds (*without joining*), unless otherwise specified. Use a small safety pin or piece of yarn in contrasting color and mark first st of rnd; move marker at beg of each rnd.

Rnd 2: Work 2 sc in each sc around = 16 sc.

Rnd 3: Rep Rnd 2 = 32 sc.

Rnd 4: Work even in sc on 32 sts.

Rnd 5: * Sc in next sc, 2 sc in next sc. Rep from * around = 48 sc.

Rnds 6 through 17: Work 12 rnds even in sc on 48 sts. At end of Rnd 17, mark top 2 lps of last sc (use marker different from beg of rnd) for working top portion of basket later.

Rnd 18: Work even in sc on 48 sts.

Rnd 19 (attachment of rings): Sc in each of next 4 sc. * Attach one ring as follows. Hold ring in front of work, aligning top of ring with working row. Working sts over top of ring, sc in each of next 10 sc (*ring attached*). * Sc in each of next 14 sc. Rep from * to * once for attachment of other ring. Sc in each rem sc around. Join with a sl st in beg sc. Lining is now completed; continue with lower outside section of basket as follows.

LOWER SECTION: Rnd 1: Ch 3, dc in next st and in each rem st around. Join with a sl st in top of beg ch-3 = 48 dc (*ch-3 counts as one dc*).

Rnds 2 through 6: Rep Rnd 1, 5 times.

Rnd 7: Ch 3, work 2 dc in next dc. * Dc in next dc, 2 dc in next dc. Rep from * around. Join with a sl st in top of beg ch-3 = 72 dc.

Rnd 8: Ch 3, dc in next st and in each rem st around. Join with a sl st in top of beg ch-3.

Rnd 9 (edging): Ch 1, sc in same st as joining. * Ch 3, sc in next dc. Rep from * around. Ch 3, join with a sl st in beg sc. Finish off; weave in ends. Push lining down inside of lower section just made. Then continue with top section of basket as follows.

TOP SECTION: Hold basket with edge next to handles at top. Work the following rnds on **Inside** of basket. Use same yarn and hook (*as for lining and lower section*) and join with a sl st in top 2 lps of marked sc.

Rnd 1: Working in top 2 lps of sts in same rnd as marked sc (*same rnd where sts of Rnd 18 of lining where worked—sc rnd before attachment of rings*), ch 3, dc in next st and in each rem st around. Join with a sl st in top of beg ch-3 = 48 dc.

Rnd 2: Ch 3, dc in same st as joining; dc in each of next 5 dc. * Work 2 dc in next dc, dc in each of next 5 dc. Rep from * around. Join with a sl st in top of beg ch-3 = 56 dc.

Rnd 3: Ch 3, dc in next dc and in each rem dc around. Join with a sl st in top of beg ch-3.

Rnds 4 and 5: Rep Rnd 3, twice.

Rnd 6 (edging): Ch 1, sc in same st as joining. * Ch 3, sc in next st. Rep from * around. Ch 3, join with a sl st in beg sc. Finish off; weave in ends. Fold last 4 rnds down to outside of basket.

PILLOW: With med pink worsted weight yarn and size J hook (*or size required to obtain gauge of 3 sc per inch*), ch 5.

Row 1: Sc in 2nd ch from hook and in each rem ch across = 4 sc.

Row 2: Ch 1, turn. Work 2 sc in each sc across = 8 sc.

Row 3: Ch 1, turn. Sc in each sc across.

Rows 4 through 15: Rep Row 3, 12 times.

Row 16: Ch 1, turn. Decrease (dec) over first 2 sc. **(To dec: Draw up a lp in each of 2 sc, YO and draw through all 3 lps on hook = dec made.)** * Dec over next 2 sc. Rep from * twice more = 4 sts. Back of pillow is now completed; work following rnds for front of pillow.

Row 17: Ch 1, turn; sc in each st across.

Rows 18 through 32: Rep Rows 2 through 16. At end of Row 32, do not finish off.

Edging and Closure: Fold work in half, keeping last row worked to outside of pillow. Carefully matching edges of front and back and corresponding rows/sts of both pieces, work (sc, ch 3) in each row/st around 3 sides. Before completing last side, lightly stuff and shape pillow. Then close last side in same manner. Join with a sl st in beg sc. Finish off; weave in ends. Place pillow inside of basket at base of lining. (*NOTE: Later, small items of layette can be kept under pillow for safe storage.*)

RIBBONS: With med pink worsted weight yarn and size J hook, make two chains: one 30″ long and the other 36″ long. Weave 36″ chain through dcs in rnd above bottom edging, beg and ending halfway between handles; tie ends into a bow. Weave 30″ chain through dcs in rnd below top edging, beg and ending at opposite end of bottom ribbon; tie ends into a bow. Knot and trim each end of chains.

DOLL

Instructions

HEAD AND BODY: Beg at top of head, with lt pink worsted weight yarn and size G hook (*or size required to obtain gauge of 4 sc per inch*), ch 4. Join with a sl st to form a ring.

Rnd 1: Work 2 sc in each ch around = 8 sc. Do not join rnds; mark first st of rnd as before.

Rnd 2: Work 2 sc **in back lp (lp away from you—Fig 1)** of each sc around = 16 sc.

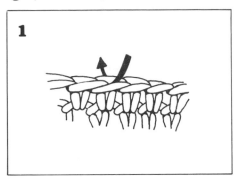

Rnd 3: Sc **in back lp** of each sc around.

Rnd 4: (marking rnd): Sc **in back lp** of next sc. In next sc, work sc in back lp and mark front lp (*use marker different from beg of rnd*) for working hair later. Sc **in back lp** of each rem sc around.

Rnds 5 and 6: Rep Rnd 3, twice. At end of Rnd 6, lightly stuff and shape head. (*NOTE: Stuffing should not be visible through sts.*)

Rnd 7: * Sk next sc, sc **in back lp** of next sc. Rep from * around = 8 sc. Head is now completed; continue with body as follows.

Rnd 8: Work 2 sc **in back lp** of each sc around = 16 sc.

Rnd 9 (marking rnd): (*NOTE: In this rnd, 2 sts are marked for sewing arms to body later.*) Sc **in back lp** of next sc. In next sc, work sc **in back lp** and mark front lp. Sc **in back lp** in each of next 7 sc. In next sc, work sc **in back lp** and mark front lp. Sc **in back lp** of each rem sc around.

Rnds 10 through 13: Rep rnd 3, 4 times. At end of Rnd 13, lightly stuff and shape body.

Rnd 14: * Sk next sc, sc **in back lp** of next sc. Rep from * around = 8 sc. Finish off, leaving approx 8″ sewing length. Thread into tapestry or yarn needle. Sew opening closed, carefully matching 4 corresponding sc across.

HAIR: Hold doll with top of head facing you. Work sts of hair in front (*unused*) lp of sts in rnds of head as follows. With brown sport weight yarn and size D hook (*or size required to obtain gauge of 5 dc per inch*), join with a sl st in st at top of head. Ch 1, sl st in same st as joining; work (sl st, ch 1, sl st) in each st in rnds around top of head, ending in marked st. Finish off; sk next 5 sts for front of face, use same yarn and hook and join with a sl st in next st. Ch 1, sl st in same st as joining; work (sl st, ch 1, sl st) in each of next 9 sts. Finish off; sk next 7 sts for front of face, use same yarn and hook and join with a sl st in next st. Ch 1, sl st in same st as joining; work (sl st, ch 1, sl st) in each of next 6 sts. Finish off; sk next 9 sts for front of face, use same yarn and hook and join with a sl st in next st. Ch 1, sl st in same st as joining; work (sl st, ch 1, sl st) in each of next 5 sts. Finish off; weave in all ends.

BOW: (optional): Cut 2 strands of yellow sport weight yarn, each 6″ long. Use crochet hook and pull both strands through st at top of head. Tie strands into a bow; trim ends evenly.

ARMS (make 2): With same yarn and hook (as for head and body), leave approx 8″ length for sewing arm to body later, ch 6. Join with a sl st to form a ring.

Rnd 1: Sc in each ch around = 6 sc. Do not join; mark first st of rnd as before.

Rnd 2: Sc **in both lps** of each sc around.

Rnds 3 through 6: Rep Rnd 2, 4 times.

Rnd 7: * Sk next sc, sl st **in both lps** of next sc. Rep from * around = 3 sl sts. Finish off; weave in end. Thread beg yarn end into tapestry or yarn needle. Sew open edge closed, carefully matching 3 corresponding sts across. Then sew this edge to side of body below marker.

FIRST LEG: Work same as arm through Rnd 6.

Rnd 7: Working in both lps of each sc, work 3 sc in next sc for front of foot, sc in each rem sc around = 8 sc.

Rnd 8: * Sk next sc, sc **in both lps** of next sc. Rep from * around = 4 sc. Finish off, leaving approx 6″ end. Thread into tapestry or yarn needle; weave through sts of last rnd. Draw up tightly and fasten securely.

SECOND LEG: Leaving approx 12″ end for sewing legs to body later, work same as first leg. Thread beg 12″ yarn end into tapestry or yarn needle. Keeping front of foot of each leg toward same side, sew open edge of 2nd leg and then first leg closed, carefully matching 3 corresponding sts of each leg across. Then sew this edge (of both legs) to bottom seam of body, keeping front of feet to front of body.

FACIAL FEATURES: Trace outlines in *Fig 2* on

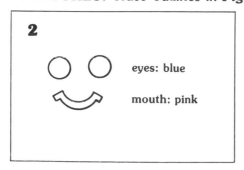

2

eyes: blue

mouth: pink

paper. Cut outlines and use as patterns on felt as indicated. With glue, attach felt pieces as shown in photo.

LAYETTE

Instructions

BONNET: With white sport weight yarn and size D hook (or size required to obtain gauge of 5 dc per inch), ch 4. Join with a sl st to form a ring.

Rnd 1: Ch 3, work 21 dc in ring. Join with a sl st in top of beg ch-3.

Rnd 2: (*NOTE: Continue by working in both lps of sts.*) Ch 3, dc in next dc and in each rem dc around. Join with a sl st in top of beg ch-3 = 22 dc (*ch-3 counts as one dc*).

Rnd 3: Ch 3, dc in each of next 2 dc, work 2 dc in next dc. * Dc in each of next 6 dc, work 2 dc in next dc. Rep from * once more. Dc in each of rem 4 dc. Join with a sl st in top of beg ch-3 = 25 dc.

Rnd 4: Ch 3, dc in next dc and in each rem dc around. Join with a sl st in top of beg ch-3.

Rnd 5: Rep Rnd 4. Finish off.

Rnd 6 (brim and ties): Turn. With inside of bonnet facing you, use same yarn and hook, ch 30 for one tie. Sk 2 dc from joining of prev rnd, sc in next dc; work (2 dc in next dc) 18 times, sc in next sc; ch 30 for other tie. Finish off (*rem sts are left unworked for back of neck*); weave in ends. Knot and trim each end of ties.

BIB: With yellow sport weight yarn and size D hook (*or size required to obtain gauge of 5 dc per inch*), ch 36.

Row 1 (right side): Sc in 2nd ch from hook; hdc in next ch, 2 dc in next ch, 3 tr (triple crochet) in next ch. Work 2 dc in next ch, hdc in next ch, sc in next ch (*leave rem chs unworked for one tie*).

Row 2: Ch 2, turn. Sk first sc, sc in next st, work (ch 2, sc) in each rem st across. Ch 2, join with a sl st in beg ch of foundation chain. Continue with same yarn and ch 29 for other tie. Finish off; knot and trim each end of ties.

BOOTIES (make 2): Beg at top, with yellow sport weight yarn and size D hook (*or size required to obtain gauge of 5 dc per inch*), ch 4. Join with a sl st to form a ring.

Rnd 1: Work 2 sc in each ch around = 8 sc. Do not join; mark first st of rnd and move marker on each following rnd.

Rnd 2: Work 2 sc **in back lp** of each sc around = 16 sc.

Rnd 3: Sc **in back lp** of each sc around.

Rnd 4: Rep Rnd 3.

Rnd 5: * Sk one sc, sc **in back lp** of next sc. Rep from * around = 8 sc.

Rnd 6 (edging): * Sc **in back lp** of next sc, ch 3. Rep from * around. Join with a sl st in beg sc. Finish off; weave in ends.

PANTIES: Beg at waist, with white sport weight yarn and size D hook (*or size required to obtain gauge of 5 dc per inch*), ch 22. Join with a sl st in beg ch to form a ring, being careful not to twist chain.

Rnd 1: Ch 1, sc in same ch as joining and in each rem ch around. Join with a sl st in beg sc = 22 sc.

Rnd 2: Ch 3, dc **in back lp** of next sc and in each rem sc around. Join with a sl st in top of beg ch-3.

Rnd 3: Ch 3, dc **in both lps** of next dc and in each rem dc around. Join with a sl st in top of beg ch-3.

Rnd 4: Ch 1, sc in same st as joining; sc **in both lps** of each rem dc around. Join with a sl st **in both lps** of beg sc.

Rnd 5: Continuing to work in both lps of each sc, ch 1, sc in same st as joining; work (sc, ch 2) in each of next 10 sts (*for leg trim*). For crotch, join next 2 sc to beg 2 sc of rnd with sl sts. Then work (ch 2, sc) in each of next 9 sts (*for other leg trim*). ch 2, join with a sl st in beg ch-1. Finish off; weave in ends.

BABY BAG: Beg at neck edge, with white sport weight yarn and size D hook (*or size required to obtain gauge of 5 dc per inch*), ch 22. Join with a sl st in beg ch to form a ring, being careful not to twist chain.

Rnd 1: Ch 1, sc in same ch as joining and in each rem ch around. Join with a sl st in beg sc = 22 sc.

Rnd 2: Working in back lp of sts (now and throughout baby bag, unless otherwise specified), ch 3, dc in next sc; 2 dc in next sc, dc in next sc; ch 5, sk 3 sc (*for arm opening*). * Dc in next sc, 2 dc in next sc. Rep from * 3 times more. Dc in next sc, ch 5, sk 3 sc (*for other arm opening*); dc in next sc, 2 dc in next sc, dc in next sc. Join with a sl st in top of beg ch-3.

Rnd 3: Ch 3, dc in next dc; dc in each rem dc and in each ch around. Join with a sl st in top of beg ch-3 = 32 dc (ch-3 counts as one dc).

Rnd 4: Ch 3, dc in next dc and in each rem dc around. Join with a sl st in top of beg ch-3.

Rnd 5: Ch 3, dc in next dc. * Work 2 dc in next dc, dc in each of next 3 dc. Rep from * to last 2 dc.

Work 2 dc in next dc, dc in last dc. Join with a sl st in top of beg ch-3 = 40 dc.

Rnds 6 through 14: Rep Rnd 4, 9 times.

Rnd 15 (beading rnd): Ch 1, sc in same st as joining * Ch 2, sk next dc, sc **in both lps** of next dc. Rep from * to last dc. Sk last dc, ch 2, join with a sl st in beg sc. Do not finish off; continue with edging up center front, around neck and then down center front as follows.

Edging: Hold work with neck edge to your left and bottom edge to your right. **Working around ch-3 of each rnd,** work (ch 2, sc) in each rnd across center front to sc rnd at neck edge. Then work (ch 2, sc) in unused lp of each ch around neck. Continuing down center front, work (ch 2, sc) around ch-3 of each rnd (*where other edging was worked*) to beading rnd at bottom edge. Ch 2, join with a sl st in beg sc of beading rnd. Finish off; weave in ends.

Drawstring: With same yarn and hook (*as in baby bag*), make a chain to measure approx 18″ long. Finish off; knot and trim each end of chain. Weave drawstring through beading rnd, beg and ending on each side of front edging.

BLANKET: With pink sport weight yarn and size D hook (*or size required to obtain gauge of 5 dc per inch*), ch 42 loosely.

Row 1: Dc in 4th ch from hook and in each rem ch across to last ch. Dc in last ch, changing to blue sport weight yarn. (**To change colors: Work st until 2 lps rem on hook; finish off color being used. With new color, YO and draw through rem 2 lps on hook = color changed.**)

Row 2: With blue, ch 3, turn. Dc in next dc and in each rem dc across; dc in top of ch-3, changing to pink sport weight yarn.

Row 3: With pink, ch 3, turn. Dc in next dc and in each rem dc across; dc in top of ch-3, changing to blue sport weight yarn.

Rep Rows 2 and 3, 5 times more. At end of last row, do not change to blue, continue with pink and work edging around all 4 sides of blanket as follows.

Edging: Working across side edge along end of rows, ch 1, work (sc, ch 2, sc) in top of end st of next row and in each rem row across. Continuing across next edge along foundation chain, work (sc, ch 2, sc, ch 2, sc) in first ch for corner. * Sk 2 chs, work (sc, ch 2, sc) in next ch. Rep from * to last 3 chs. Sk 2 chs, work (sc, ch 2, sc, ch 2, sc) in last ch for corner. Work rem 2 sides in same manner. Join with a sl st in beg sc. Finish off; weave in ends.

CLANCEY CLOWN

Designed by Eleanor Denner

Colorful Clancey has the appealing, wistful look that has made clowns children's favorites for generations.

Size

Approx 18½″ tall

Materials

American Thread Dawn Sayelle Knitting Worsted Size Yarn:
- 4 oz White
- 3 oz each of Pink and Turquoise
- 2½ oz Mod
- 1 oz Hot Orange

Size H aluminum crochet hook (or size required for gauge)

Polyester fiber (for stuffing)
Small felt pieces in red, white and black
Tracing paper and pencil
White craft glue
Size 3/0 snap (for back neck closure)

Gauge

In sc, 4 sts = 1″; 4 rows = 1″

Instructions

NOTE: Clown is worked in 2 sections (back and front) and then seamed (removable clown suit is worked later).

133

CLOWN BODY

BACK: Beg at top of head, with White, ch 9.

Row 1: Sc in 2nd ch from hook and in each rem ch across = 8 sc.

Row 2: Ch 1, turn; 2 sc in first sc, sc in each sc across to last sc, 2 sc in last sc = 10 sc.

Rows 3 through 5: Rep Row 2, 3 times = 16 sc.

Row 6: Ch 1, turn; sc in each sc across.

Rows 7 through 13: Rep Row 6, 7 times.

Row 14 (dec row): Ch 1, turn; sk first sc, sc in each sc to last 2 sc; sk next sc, sc in last sc = 14 sc.

Rows 15 through 18: Rep Row 14, 4 times. At end of Row 18, you should have 6 sc.

Row 19: Rep Row 6.

Row 20: Ch 26 (for arm), turn; sc in 2nd ch from hook and in each rem ch and sc across = 31 sc.

Row 21: Rep Row 20 = 56 sc.

Rows 22 through 24: Rep Row 6, 3 times.

Row 25: Ch 1, turn; sc in each of first 36 sc (leave rem sts unworked for arm).

Row 26: Ch 1, turn; sc in each of first 16 sc (leave rem sts unworked for other arm). Continue working on 16 sts only for body as follows.

Rows 27 through 42: Rep Row 6, 16 times.

Row 43: Rep Row 14 = 14 sc. Do not finish off; continue with left leg and shoe as follows.

LEFT LEG AND SHOE: Row 1: Ch 1, turn; sc in each of first 7 sc (leave rem sts unworked for working right leg later).

Row 2 (dec row): Ch 1, turn; sk first sc, sc in each rem sc across = 6 sc.

Row 3: Ch 1, turn; sc in each sc across.

Rows 4 through 23: Rep Row 3, 20 times. **At end of Row 23, change to Pink (for shoe) in last sc. [To change color: Work last sc until 2 lps rem on hook, finish off White; tie in Pink (leave ends on inside of clown) and complete st (YO and draw through both lps on hook) = color changed.]**

Row 24: With Pink, rep Row 3.

Row 25: Ch 15 (for front of shoe), turn; sc in 2nd ch from hook and in each rem ch and sc across = 20 sc.

Rows 26 through 31: Rep Row 3, 6 times.

At end of Row 31, finish off and weave in ends.

RIGHT LEG AND SHOE: Hold clown with leg just worked at top and to your right. Join White with a sl st in sc next to left leg.

Row 1: Ch 1, sc in same st as joining and in each rem sc across = 7 sc.

Row 2 (dec row): Ch 1, turn; sc in each sc across to last 2 sc; sk next sc, sc in last sc = 6 sc.

Row 3: Ch 1, turn; sc in each sc across.

Rows 4 through 23: Rep Row 3, 20 times. At end of Row 23, finish off White; continue by working shoe as follows.

Row 24: Turn; with Turquoise, ch 14 (for front of shoe), sc in each sc across.

Row 25: Ch 1, turn; sc in each sc and ch across = 20 sc.

Rows 26 through 31: Rep Row 3, 6 times.

At end of Row 31, finish off and weave in ends.

FRONT: Work same as Back.

ASSEMBLING: Hold Front and Back sections tog, matching arms, legs and shoes. Thread tapestry or yarn needle with strand of White. Carefully matching sts and rows around, and stuffing arms and head as sections are joined, sew sections tog with overcast st around outside White edges (*working up, around, and then down*), ending at other ankle. Stuff body and then sew inside edges of legs tog. Now stuff legs and join rem edges of each shoe tog as follows: Leaving toe edge open, use matching yarn and sew rem edges closed; stuff shoe and sew toe opening closed as shown in *Fig 1.*

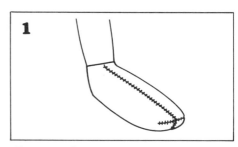

HAIR: First read *Basic Hair Instructions* below. With Hot Orange, work 1″ loop sts across back of head as follows: Hold clown with back facing you and head at top. Beg at side seam to your left in 5th row from seam at top of head. Working across between side seams and down toward neck, work 6 rows of lp sts, having first and last st of each row worked around side seam.

FACIAL FEATURES: Trace outlines in *Fig 2* on paper. Cut outlines and use as patterns on felt as indicated. (*NOTE: To prevent pattern pieces from slipping on felt, tape pieces in place with cellophane tape. Cut felt pieces through tape and then discard tape.*) With glue, attach felt pieces as shown in photo. For nose, make ½″ diameter Pink pompon (see page 11) and attach to center of face.

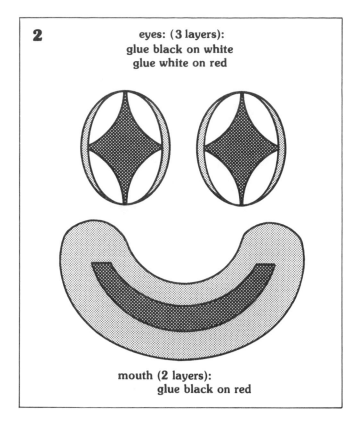

2

eyes: (3 layers):
glue black on white
glue white on red

mouth (2 layers):
glue black on red

CLOWN SUIT

NOTE: Suit is worked in 4 identical sections; then seamed.

SECTION (make 2 each of Turquoise and Pink — 4 total): Beg at ankle, ch 11.

Row 1: Hdc in 3rd ch from hook and in each rem ch across = 9 hdc. (NOTE: Throughout patt, do not count ch-2 as one st.)

Row 2: Ch 2, turn; hdc in each of first 2 hdc, * 2 hdc in next hdc, hdc in each of next 2 hdc; rep from * once more, 2 hdc in last hdc = 12 hdc.

Row 3: Ch 2, turn; hdc in each hdc across.

Rows 4 through 10: Rep Row 3, 7 times.

Row 11: Ch 2, turn; 2 hdc in first hdc, hdc in each rem hdc across = 13 hdc.

Rows 12 through 14: Rep Row 3, 3 times.

Row 15: Rep Row 11 = 14 hdc. Mark last st worked (use small safety pin or piece of yarn in contrasting color) for sewing sections tog later (identifies crotch).

Rows 16 through 18: Rep Row 3, 3 times.

Row 19: Rep Row 11 = 15 hdc.

Rows 20 through 26: Rep Row 3, 7 times.

Row 27: Ch 9 (for sleeve), turn; sc in 2nd ch from hook, hdc in each rem ch and hdc across = 23 sts.

Row 28: Ch 2, turn; hdc in each hdc across to last sc, sc in last sc.

Row 29: Ch 1, turn; sc in first sc, hdc in each hdc across.

Rows 30 through 32: Rep Rows 28 and 29 once, then rep Row 28 once more.

Row 33: Ch 1, turn; sc in first sc, hdc in each of next 18 hdc (leave rem 4 hdc unworked for neck edge) = 19 sts.

Row 34: Rep Row 28.

Finish off and weave in ends.

ASSEMBLING: (NOTE: For front and back, right half of suit is Pink and left half is Turquoise.) For front, place one Pink section and one Turquoise section side by side, matching straight edges at center. Beg at neck and sew center edges tog with overcast st (carefully matching rows) to marker at crotch. For back, sew rem 2 sections tog in same manner, leaving approx 3″ free from neck edge for back opening. Now hold front and back pieces tog, matching arms and legs. Sew shoulder, sleeve, side and leg seams.

NECK RUFFLE: Hold suit with back facing you and neck edge at top. Join Mod with a sl st in st at left back center neck edge.

Row 1: Ch 1, sc in same st as joining and in each of next 3 hdc; sc in each of next 4 rows (2 rows on each side of shoulder seam), sc in each of next 8 hdc across front; sc in each of next 4 rows, sc in each of next 4 hdc, ending at right back neck edge = 24 sc.

Row 2: Ch 1, turn; * sk next sc, sc in next sc; rep from * across = 12 sc.

Row 3: Ch 3 (counts as one dc), turn; working **in front lp** (lp toward you) of each st, 2 dc in first sc, 3 dc in each rem sc across = 36 dc. Continue by working **in both lps** of sts.

Row 4: Ch 3, turn; dc in first dc, 2 dc in each rem dc across, ending by working 2 dc in top of ch-3 = 72 dc.

Row 5: Ch 3, turn; sk first dc, * sc in next dc, ch 3; rep from * across, ending by working sl st in top of ch-3 = 71 ch-3 sps.

Finish off and weave in ends. Tack each end of ruffle to side edge of back opening. With sewing thread, sew snap at back neck opening for closure.

SLEEVE RUFFLES (make 2): With sleeve edge across top, join Mod with a sl st in first row to left of underarm seam.

Rnd 1: Ch 1, sc in same row as joining and in each row around sleeve edge, join with a sl st in beg sc = 16 sc.

Rnd 2: Ch 1, **Do not turn;** 2 sc **in front lp** of each sc around, join with a sl st in beg sc = 32 sc. Continue by working **in both lps** of sts.

Rnd 3: Ch 4, **Do not turn;** sc in first sc, * ch 3, sc in next sc; rep from * around, ch 3, join with a sl st in first ch of beg ch-4 = 32 ch-3 sps.

Finish off and weave in ends.

LEG RUFFLES (make 2): With leg edge across top, join Mod with a sl st in first st to left of inside leg seam.

Rnd 1: Ch 1, sc in same st as joining and in each rem st around, join with a sl st in beg sc = 18 sc.

Rnd 2: Ch 3 (counts as one dc), **Do not turn;** working **in front lp** of each st, 2 dc in first sc, 3 dc in each rem sc around; join with a sl st in top of beg ch-3 = 54 dc. Continue by working **in both lps** of sts.

Rnd 3: Ch 4, **Do not turn;** sc in first sc, * ch 3, sc in next sc; rep from * around, ch 3, join with a sl st in first ch of beg ch-4 = 54 ch-3 sps.

Finish off and weave in ends.

POMPONS: With Mod, make two 1½″ diameter pompons (*see page 11*). Attach pompons evenly spaced down center front of suit as shown in photo.

BASIC HAIR INSTRUCTIONS

Hair is sewn onto head with loop sts as follows:

STEP 1: Cut approx 72″ strand of yarn; fold strand in half. Thread into tapestry or yarn needle doubled, having folded end at farthest end from needle (*Fig 1*).

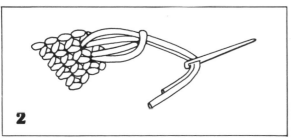

STEP 2 (joining): Insert needle around st (*from right to left*); pull yarn through, bringing needle up through folded end (*Fig 2*). Pull up tightly to secure.

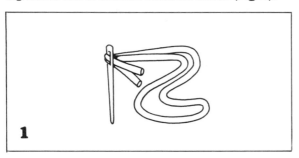

STEP 3: (*NOTE: First loop st is worked around same st as joining.*) Insert needle around st (*from right to left as before*); pull yarn through, leaving approx 1″ slack loop (or length of loop specified in patt instructions) on left index finger (*Fig 3*).

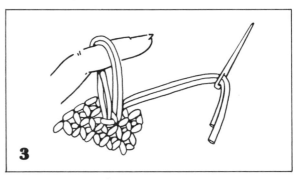

STEP 4: Keeping loop on left index finger, insert needle around same st again (*from right to left*) and pull yarn through. Pull up tightly to secure.

STEP 5: Drop loop off left index finger (*one loop st made*).

Working to your right, rep Steps 3 through 5 around each st (*as specified in patt instructions*), until a new sewing length is needed. Cut yarn, leaving approx ½″ ends to fall in as part of hair. Then beg again with Step 1 and continue working loop sts in this manner until hair is completed.

BROTHER AND SISTER DOLLS

These curly-top twins are sure to be a young child's favorite companions. Soft but sturdy, the dolls can be made with your choice of skin and hair color.

Size

Each doll measures approx 14″ tall

Materials

American Thread Dawn Sayelle Knitting Worsted Size Yarn:
>   4 oz each of Royal Blue, Cinnamon and Black
>   3½ oz Spirit of 76
>   ½ oz White

Size H aluminum crochet hook (or size required for gauge)
Polyester fiber (for stuffing)
Small felt pieces in white, black and red
Tracing paper and pencil
White craft glue
2 White button (¼″ diameter)

Gauge

In sc, 4 sts = 1″; 4 rnds = 1″

BROTHER

Instructions

NOTE: Throughout patt, unless otherwise specified, work all rnds on right side; do not turn at beg of rnds.

HEAD: Beg at top, with Cinnamon, ch 4, join with a sl st to form a ring.

Rnd 1: Work 6 sc in ring, join with a sl st in beg sc. (NOTE: Throughout patt, unless otherwise specified, join all rnds in this manner.)

Rnd 2: Ch 1, 2 sc in same st as joining, 2 sc in each rem sc around, join (as before) = 12 sc.

Rnd 3: Ch 1, sc in same st as joining, 2 sc in next sc; * sc in next sc, 2 sc in next sc; rep from * around, join = 18 sc.

Rnd 4: Ch 1, sc in same st as joining, sc in next sc, 2 sc in next sc; * sc in each of next 2 sc, 2 sc in next sc; rep from * around, join = 24 sc.

Rnd 5: Ch 1, sc in same st as joining and in each rem sc around, join. (NOTE: On following rnds, when instructions say to "work even", work same as rnd 5.)

Rnd 6: Work even.

Rnd 7: Ch 1, sc in same st as joining, sc in each of next 4 sc, 2 sc in next sc; * sc in each of nxt 5 sc, 2 sc in next sc; rep from * around, join = 28 sc.

Rnd 8: Ch 1, sc in same st as joining, sc in each of next 5 sc, 2 sc in next sc; * sc in each of next 6 sc, 2 sc in next sc; rep from * around, join = 32 sc.

Rnd 9: Ch 1, sc in same st as joining, sc in each of next 6 sc, 2 sc in next sc; * sc in each of next 7 sc, 2 sc in next sc; rep from * around, join = 36 sc.

Rnds 10 through 14: Work 5 rnds even.

Rnd 15 (dec rnd): Ch 1, sc in same st as joining; sc in each of next 4 sc, sk one sc; * sc in each of next 5 sc, sk one sc; rep from * around, join = 30 sc.

Rnd 16 (dec rnd): Ch 1, sc in same st as joining; sc in each of next 3 sc, sk one sc; * sc in each of next 4 sc, sk one sc; rep from * around, join = 24 sc.

Rnd 17: Rep Rnd 15 = 20 sc.

Rnd 18: Rep Rnd 16 = 16 sc.

Rnd 19: Work even. At end of rnd, change to Royal Blue in joining sl st. [To change color: Insert hook in beg sc; finish off Cinnamon, tie in Royal Blue (leave ends on inside of doll); continuing with Royal Blue, YO and pull through st and lp on hook = color changed.] Lightly stuff and shape head; then continue with shirt as follows.

SHIRT: Rnd 1: With Royal Blue, work even = 16 sc.

Rnd 2: Ch 1, sc in same st as joining, sc in each of next 2 sc, 2 sc in next sc, * sc in each of next 3 sc, 2 sc in next sc; rep from * around; join, changing to Spirit of 76 (in same manner as before) = 20 sc.

Rnd 3: With Spirit of 76, work even.

Rnd 4: Ch 1, sc in same st as joining, sc in in each of next 3 sc, 2 sc in next sc; * sc in each of next 4 sc, 2 sc in next sc; rep from * around, join = 24 sc.

Rnd 5 (marking rnd): (NOTE: In this rnd, 2 sts are

marked for attaching sleeves later.) Ch 1, sc in same st as joining, sc in each of next 5 sc; sc in next sc and mark st just made (use small safety pin or piece of yarn in contrasting color); sc in each of next 10 sc, sc in next sc and mark st just made; sc in each of rem 6 sc, join.

Rnd 6: Ch 1, sc in same st as joining, sc in each of next 2 sc, 2 sc in next sc; * sc in each of next 3 sc, 2 sc in next sc; rep from * around, join = 30 sc.

Rnd 7: Rep Rnd 4 = 36 sc.

Rnds 8 through 15: Work 8 rnds even.

At end of Rnd 15, change to Royal Blue in joining sl st; then continue with pants as follows.

PANTS: Rnd 1: With Royal Blue, work even = 36 sc.

Rnd 2: Ch 1, sc in same st as joining, sc in each of next 2 sc; sc **in back lp** (lp away from you) in each of next 2 sc (front lps will be used later to work strap), sc **in both lps** in each of next 10 sc, sc **in back lp** in each of next 9 sc (front lps will be used later to work bib); sc **in both lps** in each of next 8 sc, sc **in back lp** in each of next 2 sc (front lps will be used later to work other strap); sc **in both lps** in each of rem 2 sc, join. (NOTE: Continue by working in **both lps** of sts.)

Rnds 3 through 10: Work 8 rnds even.

At end of Rnd 10, lightly stuff and shape body, then continue with left pant leg and shoe as follows.

LEFT PANT LEG AND SHOE: Rnd 1: Ch 1, sc in same st as joining, 2 sc in next sc, mark next sc for working right leg later; sk st just marked and next 17 sc (18 sts total—for working right pant leg later): 2 sc in next sc, sc in each of rem 15 sc, join = 20 sc.

Rnd 2: Work even.

Rnd 3: Ch 1, sc in same st as joining, sc in next sc; dec over next 2 sc. **To make dec: Draw up a lp in each of next 2 sc, YO and draw through all 3 lps on hook (dec made):** sc in each of rem 16 sc, join = 19 sc.

Rnds 4 through 14: Work 11 rnds even.

At end of Rnd 14, change to Black in joining sl st (for working shoe).

Rnd 15: With Black, work even.

Rnd 16: Ch 1, sc in same st as joining; * sc in next sc, 2 sc in next sc; rep from * around, join = 28 sc.

Rnds 17 and 18: Work 2 rnds even.

Rnd 19: Ch 1, sc in same st as joining, sk one sc; * sc in next sc, sk one sc; rep from * around, join = 14 sc.

Lightly stuff and shape leg and shoe.

Rnd 20: Rep Rnd 19 = 7 sc.

Finish off, leaving approx 6″ end. Thread into tapestry or yarn needle; weave through sts of last rnd. Draw up tightly and fasten securely.

RIGHT PANT LEG AND SHOE: Rnd 1: Hold doll with leg just worked at top and to your right. With Royal Blue, make a slip knot on hook; join with a sc in marked st at crotch, sc in each of next 17 sc around leg opening; sc in each of next 2 sts at crotch, join = 20 sc.

Rnd 2: Work even.

Rnd 3: Ch 1, sc in same st as joining, sc in each of next 17 sc; dec over last 2 sc, join = 19 sc.

Rnds 4 through 20: Work same as Left Pant Leg and Shoe.

ARM AND SLEEVE (make 2): Beg at hand, with Cinnamon, ch 3, join with a sl st to form a ring.

Rnd 1: Work 7 sc in ring, join.

Rnd 2: Ch 1, sc in same st as joining, 2 sc in each rem sc around, join = 13 sc.

Rnds 3 through 14: Work 12 rnds even.

At end of Rnd 14, change to Royal Blue in joining sl st (for working sleeve trim).

Rnds 15 and 16: With Royal Blue, work 2 rnds even.

At end of Rnd 16, change to Spirit of 76 in joining sl st (for sleeve).

Rnd 17: With Spirit of 76, ch 1, sk first sc (same st as joining), sl st in each of next 2 sc, ch 1; * sc in next sc, 2 sc in next sc; rep from * 4 times more, sc in beg ch-1, **Do not join** = 16 sc. Continue by working back and forth in rows as follows:

> **Row 1:** Ch 1, turn; dec over first 2 sc, sc in each of next 12 sc, dec over last 2 sc = 14 sc.
>
> **Row 2:** Ch 1, turn; dec over first 2 sc, sc in each sc across to last 2 sc, dec = 12 sc.
>
> **Rows 3 and 4:** Rep Row 2 (prev row), twice.
> At end of Row 4, you should have 8 sc.

Finish off, leaving approx 16″ sewing length. Lightly stuff and shape arm and sleeve. Pin sleeve edge to side of shirt, having center top at marker and underarm approx 4 rnds up from waist. Thread sewing length into tapestry or yarn needle and sew sleeve in place.

BIB: Hold doll with head at top and side with 9 unused (front) lps of sts at waist facing you.

Row 1: With Royal Blue, make a slip knot on hook; join with a sc in first (unused) lp to your right (insert hook under lp from bottom to top of doll); sc in each of next 8 lps = 9 sc.

Row 2: Ch 1, turn; sc in each sc across.

Rows 3 through 9: Rep Row 2, 7 times.

At end of Row 9, finish off; weave in ends.

STRAPS (make 2): Hold doll with head away from you and 2 unused (front) lps of sts at waist facing you.

Row 1: With Royal Blue, make a slip knot on hook; join with a sc in first lp to your right, sc in next lp = 2 sc.

Row 2: Ch 1, turn; sc in each sc across. Rep Row 2 until strap measures approx 6″ long.

Finish off, leaving approx 12″ sewing length; thread into tapestry or yarn needle. Having straps crossed at back, sew end of strap to bib, overlapping 2 top rows of bib. With matching sewing thread, sew one button at end of strap through both thicknesses of strap and bib.

HAIR: *Follow Basic Hair Instructions* under "Clancey Clown" on page 136

With Black, work loop sts around head to establish hairline as follows: Hold doll with back facing you and legs at top. Beg in 4th rnd from shirt where rnd was joined and work 6 sts (*each approx 1″ long*) across back of neck. Then work 4 sts up on a diagonal to side of head (align side of head with center of shoulder, leaving approx 16 sts free across front for face). Continuing up side of head, work one st in each rnd to within 3 rnds from top. In 3rd rnd from top, work one st in each st across front to opposite side. Complete hairline around head to correspond to other side. Next, fill in hair inside of hairline; beg at top and work sts back and forth in rows.

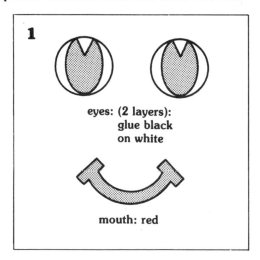

eyes: (2 layers): glue black on white

mouth: red

FACIAL FEATURES: Trace outlines in *Fig 1*, on paper. Cut outlines and use as patterns on felt as indicated. (*NOTE: To prevent pattern pieces from slipping on felt, tape pieces in place with cellophane tape. Cut felt pieces through tape and then discard tape.*) With glue, attach felt pieces as shown in photo.

SISTER

Instructions

NOTE: Throughout patt, unless otherwise specified, work all rnds on right side; do not turn at beg of rnds.

HEAD: Work same as Brother.

At end of Rnd 19, change to White (instead of Royal Blue) in joining sl st. Lightly stuff and shape head; then continue with blouse as follows.

BLOUSE: Rnd 1: With White, work even = 16 sc.

Rnd 2: Ch 1, sc in same st as joining, sc in each of next 2 sc, 2 sc in next sc; * sc in each of next 3 sc, 2 sc in next sc; rep from * around; join, changing to Royal Blue = 20 sc.

Rnds 3 through 15: With Royal Blue, rep Rnds 3 through 15 of Shirt instructions for Brother.

At end of Rnd 15, do not finish off Royal Blue; continue with panties as follows.

PANTIES: Rnd 1: With Royal Blue, ch 1, sc **in back lp** (lp away from you) in same sc as joining; sc **in back lp** in each rem sc around, join = 36 sc. (*NOTE: Front lps will be used later to work skirt.*) Continue by working **in both lps** of sts.

Rnds 2 through 10: Work 9 rnds even.

At end of Rnd 10, lightly stuff and shape body; then continue with left leg, sock and shoe as follows.

LEFT LEG, SOCK AND SHOE: Rnd 1: With Royal Blue, ch 1, sc in same st as joining, 2 sc in next sc, *mark next sc for working right leg later;* sk st just marked and next 17 sc (*18 sts total—for working right leg later*); 2 sc in next sc, sc in each of rem 15 sc; join, changing to Cinnamon = 20 sc.

Rnd 2: With Cinnamon, work even.

Rnd 3: Ch 1, sc in same st as joining, sc in next sc, dec over next 2 sc. **To make dec: Draw up a lp in each of next 2 sc, YO and draw through all 3 lps on hook (dec made);** sc in each of rem 16 sc, join = 19 sc.

Rnds 4 through 10: Work 7 rnds even.

At end of Rnd 10, change to White in joining sl st (for sock trim).

Rnd 11: With White, work even.

At end of rnd, change to Royal Blue in joining sl st (for sock).

Rnds 12 through 14: With Royal Blue, work 3 rnds even.

At end of Rnd 14, change to Black in joining sl st (for shoe).

Rnds 15 through 20: Rep Rnds 15 through 20 of Left Pant Leg and Shoe instructions for Brother.

RIGHT LEG, SOCK AND SHOE: Rnd 1: Hold doll with leg just worked at top and to your right. With Royal Blue, make a slip knot on hook; join with a sc in marked st at crotch, sc in each of next 17 sc around leg opening, sc in each of next 2 sts at crotch; join, changing to Cinnamon = 20 sc.

Rnd 2: With Cinnamon, work even.

Rnd 3: Ch 1, sc in same st as joining, sc in each of next 17 sc; dec over last 2 sc, join = 19 sc.

Rnds 4 through 20: Work same as Left Leg, Sock and Shoe.

SKIRT: Rnd 1: Hold doll with back facing you (side where rnds were joined) and legs at top. With Spirit of 76, make a slip knot on hook. *Working in unused (front) lp of sts left unworked in first rnd of panties,* join with a sc in st at center back, sc in each rem st around, join = 36 sc.

Rnd 2: Ch 3, do not turn. Working **in back lp** of each st around, dc in same st as joining, 2 dc in each rem sc around; join with a sl st in top of beg ch-3 = 72 dc (*counting beg ch-3*). (*NOTE: Front lp of sts will be used later to work edging around waist of skirt*). Continue by working **in both lps** of sts.

Rnd 3: Ch 3, do not turn; dc in next dc and in each rem dc around, join with a sl st in top of beg ch-3.

Rnds 4 through 7: Rep Rnd 3, 4 times.

At end of Rnd 7, finish off and weave in ends; then work edging around waist edge of skirt as follows.

EDGING: Hold doll with back facing you and head at top. With Spirit of 76, make a slip knot on hook.

Rnd 1: Working in unused (*front*) lp of sts left unworked in first rnd of skirt, join with a sc in st at center back; sc in each rem st around, join = 36 sc.

Rnd 2: Work even.

Finish off; weave in ends.

ARM AND SLEEVE (make 2): Beg at hand, with Cinnamon, ch 3, join with a sl st to form a ring.

Rnds 1 through 14: Work same as Brother.

At end of Rnd 14, change to White in joining sl st (instead of Royal Blue) for working sleeve trim.

Rnds 15 and 16: With White, work 2 rnds even.

At end of Rnd 16, change to Royal Blue (for sleeve) in joining sl st.

Rnd 17: With Royal Blue, ch 1, sk first sc (same st as joining), sl st in each of next 2 sc; ch 1, sc in next sc, 2 sc in each of next 9 sc, sc in beg ch-1; **Do not join** = 20 sc. Continue by working back and forth in rows as follows:

Row 1: Ch 1, turn, dec over first 2 sc, sc in each of next 16 sc, dec over last 2 sc = 18 sc.

Row 2: Ch 1, turn; dec over first 2 sc, sc in each sc across to last 2 sc, dec over last 2 sc = 16 sc.

Row 3: Rep Row 2 = 14 sc.

Row 4: Ch 1, turn; * dec over next 2 sc; rep from * 6 times more = 7 sc.

Finish off, leaving approx 16″ sewing length. Lightly stuff and shape arm and sleeve. Sew sleeve to side of blouse in same manner as Brother.

SKIRT STRAPS (make 2): With Spirit of 76, leave approx 6″ end for sewing strap to skirt later, make a chain to measure approx 6″ long. Finish off, leaving approx 6″ sewing length. Having right side of chain facing doll, sew one end of strap to back of skirt under edging, leaving 3 sts free between straps. Sew opposite end of strap to front of skirt under edging, having straps crossed at back and leaving 6 sts free between straps at front.

HAIR: Work same as Brother, having each loop st measure approx 1½″ long (instead of 1″ long).

HAIR BOW: With White, make a chain to measure approx 7″ long. Finish off; knot and trim each end of chain. Tie chain into a bow around base of one loop st of hair at center front.

FACIAL FEATURES: Work same as Brother.

MOUSE TOY

designed by Mary Thomas

Don't leave the family cat out of the holiday festivities! Make this delightful toy mouse to put in kitty's Christmas stocking.

Size

Approx 3½″ body length

Materials

Sport weight yarn:
    ½ oz gray
    few yds pink
Aluminum crochet hook size D (or size required for gauge)
Yarn scraps for stuffing

Gauge

In sc, 5 sts = 1″; 6 rnds = 1″

Instructions

BODY: With gray beg at head, ch 2.

Rnd 1: Work 6 sc in 2nd ch from hook, join with a sl st in beg sc.

NOTE: On all following rnds: At beg of each rnd, ch 1 and turn; at end of each rnd, join with a sl st in beg sc.

Rnd 2: Work 2 sc in each sc around = 12 sc.

Rnd 3: Sc in each of first 3 sc, 2 sc in next sc, * sc in next sc, 2 sc in next sc; rep from * around = 17 sc.

Rnd 4: Work 2 sc in first sc, sc in each of next 12 sc, 2 sc in next sc, sc in each of last 3 sc = 19 sc.

Rnd 5: Sc in each sc around.

Rnds 6 and 7: Rep Rnd 5 twice.

Rnd 8: Sc in each of first 8 sc, * work 2 sc in next sc, sc in each of next 2 sc; rep from * once, 2 sc in next sc, sc in each of rem 4 sc = 22 sc.

Rnds 9 through 13: Rep Rnd 5 five times.

Rnd 14: Sc in each of first 6 sc, work a sc dec over next 2 sc, sc in each sc to last 2 sc, dec as before = 20 sc.

Rnd 15: Rep Rnd 5.

Rnd 16: Rep Rnd 14 = 18 sc.

Rnd 17: Rep Rnd 5.

Rnd 18: Sc in each of first 5 sc, dec; sc in each of next 4 sc, dec; sc in each of next 3 sc, dec over last 2 sc = 15 sc.

Rnd 19: Rep Rnd 5. Before working next rnd, stuff body with yarn scraps.

Rnd 20: * Dec, sc in next sc, rep from * around = 10 sc.

Rnd 21: Rep Rnd 5. Do not finish off.

TAIL: Continuing with same yarn, make a ch to measure approx 6″. Sl st **loosely** in 2nd ch from hook and in each rem ch across. Finish off, leaving approx 6″ sewing length. Thread yarn into tapestry needle and sew end of body closed, then secure tail to body. With pink make a ch approx 12″ long and tie on tail for bow.

EARS (*make 2*): With pink, beg by leaving 8″ sewing length, ch 4.

Row 1: Sc in 2nd ch from hook and in each rem ch across = 3 sc.

NOTE: On all following rows: Ch 1 and turn to beg each row.

Row 2: Work 2 sc in each sc across = 6 sc.

Row 3: Work 2 sc in first sc, sc in each of next 4 sc, 2 sc in last sc = 8 sc.

Row 4: Sc in each sc across.

Row 5: Dec, sc in each of next 4 sc, dec = 6 sc.

Row 6: Dec, sc in each of next 2 sc, dec = 4 sc.

Row 7: Dec twice = 2 sc.

Finish off and weave in this yarn end. Thread beg yarn end into tapestry needle and attach to body.

EMBROIDERY: With pink, embroider several satin sts over Rnd 1 of Body for nose and one French knot for each eye.